£45 £12.99

Wellington's Army

Greenhill Books

COSTUME of the BRITISH ARMY.

&c. &c. &c.

Wellington's Army

The Uniforms of the British Soldier, 1812–1815

PLATES BY

Charles Hamilton Smith

TEXT BY

Philip J. Haythornthwaite

Greenhill Books, London
Stackpole Books, Pennsylvania

The publishers would like to thank the Anne S.K. Brown Military Collection
(all plates except No. 39) and the Director of the National Army Museum, London (Plate 39)
for granting permission to reproduce the plates of Charles Hamilton Smith in this volume.
The Military Collection is housed in the John Hay Library of Brown University,
Providence, Rhode Island, USA.

Wellington's Army is a companion volume to *Napoleon's Elite Cavalry:*
Cavalry of the Imperial Guard, 1804-1815 (The Paintings of Lucien Rousselot),
which has text by Edward Ryan, and is also published by Greenhill Books.

Wellington's Army
first published in 2002 by
Greenhill Books, Lionel Leventhal Limited,
Park House, 1 Russell Gardens, London NW11 9NN
and
Stackpole Books, 5067 Ritter Road,
Mechanicsburg, PA 17055, USA

British Library Cataloguing in Publication Data
Smith, Charles Hamilton
Wellington's army: uniforms of the British soldier, 1812–1815
1. Great Britain. Army – Uniforms 2. Peninsular War, 1807–1814 – Great Britain
3. Waterloo, Battle of, 1815 – Great Britain
I. Title II. Haythornthwaite, Philip J. (Philip John), 1951–
355.1'4'0942'09034

ISBN 1-85367-501-6

Library of Congress Cataloging-in-Publication Data
A catalog record is available from the library.

Typeset and edited by Donald Sommerville.

Printed in Thailand by Imago

Contents

Artillery, Engineers, Transport and Other Services   121

Foreign Regiments and the Militia of Great Britain and Ireland   137

Royal Marines, Cadets and Other British Subjects   153

Troops of the East India Company   163

number of squadrons, each of two troops, these being the principal formations for manoeuvre. From 1811 line regiments generally comprised three 'service' squadrons, with a fourth remaining at home as the regimental depot; Light Dragoons comprised five squadrons, increased to six in September 1813, of which one acted as a depot. Regimental strength, especially on campaign, was often lower than the official establishment, and was usually only about 400 men; for example, strengths of the regiments at Salamanca varied from 273 of all ranks to 407, averaging 354; at Waterloo (excluding the under-strength Household units) from 341 to 712, averaging 471 (average 433 if the very strong King's German Legion units are excluded).

The Household Cavalry consisted of the two regiments of Life Guards (Plates 6 and 7), the senior regiments in the army, and traditionally the sovereign's bodyguard. Although not officially part of the Household Cavalry until March 1820, the Royal Horse Guards (or 'Blues') were regarded virtually as such (Plate 8). They had served in the Netherlands in 1794, but otherwise the Household regiments remained at home until it was decided in 1812 to send to the Peninsula two squadrons each of the two Life Guard regiments, and the Blues; they served there from early 1813. Similarly, two squadrons each of the Life Guard regiments, and the Royal Horse Guards and 1st Dragoon Guards, constituted a brigade in the Waterloo campaign. The remaining Household squadrons were kept at home to perform ceremonial duties.

The heavy cavalry comprised the Dragoon Guards and Dragoons, virtually indistinguishable except for title and minor aspects of uniform. The appellation 'Dragoon Guard' did not imply 'Guard' status in the conventional sense of a royal bodyguard, but was a title used simply to identify those senior regiments which prior to 1746 had been titled 'Horse'. The five Dragoon regiments were numbered 1st–4th and 6th, the rank of the 5th being the only vacant number in the *Army List*. Usually, upon the disbandment of a regiment, those bearing higher numbers would be renumbered; but the gap in the list of dragoon regiments was left deliberately, following the disbandment of the 5th Dragoons, as a punishment, in 1799, as described in the text to Plate 23.

The regiments of Light Dragoons were numbered in sequence after the 6th Dragoons; at the period in question, these numbers ran from 7 to 25, of which four regiments – the 7th, 10th, 15th and 18th – had the additional title of Hussars, and were uniformed accordingly (Plates 13, 15, 18 and 19). In theory the light regiments were intended for skirmishing and 'outpost' duty in addition to their role as a striking-force on the battlefield, the latter traditionally the main role of the heavy cavalry; but unlike the situation in some continental armies, the British cavalry was not sufficiently numerous for such distinctions to be observed at all times, so that from force of circumstances, in the Peninsula ostensibly 'heavy' regiments had to become almost as versatile as the light cavalry.

Although they carried firearms with which to skirmish (see Plate 18), the cavalry's principal weapon was the sword. The heavy and light cavalry patterns of 1796 were carried from about that date, the heavy cavalry sabre with a straight blade (shown in Plates 6–11) and that of the light cavalry, curved. They were designed under the direction of John Gaspard Le Marchant (see text to Plate 54) when experience in the early French Revolutionary Wars had revealed the imperfections in the earlier patterns, and they remained in use for the remainder of the period. Though a considerable improvement on former types, they were not beyond criticism: the heavy cavalry sabre, for example, was described as:

> 'a lumbering, clumsy, ill-contrived machine. It is too heavy, too short, too broad, and too much like the sort of weapon with which we have seen Grimaldi cut off the heads of a line or urchins on the stage.'[3]

3. *Ibid.* 1831, Vol. II, p. 61.

Both types of sword were designed to execute the cut or slash and, despite the criticism, could be brutally effective, as described by Charles Ewart of the 2nd Dragoons in his account of the capture of a French Eagle at Waterloo. He was engaged by three Frenchmen; the first 'thrust for my groin – I parried it off, and cut him through the head', the next 'I cut him from the chin upwards, which cut went through his teeth', and the third 'charged me with his bayonet... I parried it and cut him down through the head.'[4]

The Infantry

At the period in question, the infantry comprised three regiments of Foot Guards and 104 numbered line regiments, each with its own colonel, identity and traditions. Unlike the cavalry, the infantry's principal tactical unit was not the regiment, but the battalion. Although some regiments consisted of only a single battalion, many had two or more. At the beginning of the Peninsular War, for example, of the 103 line regiments then existing (the New Brunswick Fencibles was taken into the line as the 104th only in 1810), 61 had two battalions, the 14th and 17th Foot three each, and the 1st Foot, four; excluding the 60th and 95th (covered below), the remaining 37 had but one battalion. A number of regiments raised additional battalions subsequently. Each battalion comprised ten companies, eight 'battalion' or 'centre' companies, and two 'flank' companies (these terms deriving from the position of the companies when drawn up in line). One flank company was composed of grenadiers, supposedly the largest and most stalwart individuals, and the other of light infantry, nimble men trained in skirmishing.

It was intended originally that, for regiments with two battalions, one should go on active service and the other remain at home, to act as the regimental depot and provide a source of reinforcements for the 'service' battalion. Before a battalion embarked on active service, it exchanged its least effective men for others from the 'home' battalion, so that when the 2nd Battalion was also ordered on service, as frequently happened, it would be considerably weaker by having to leave behind not only its own 'ineffective' men but also those of the 1st Battalion.

Only rarely did a battalion achieve the notional strength of 1,000 men (100 per company). At Salamanca, for example, battalion-strengths ranged from 1,079 (1/42nd) to 251 (2/44th) of all ranks; 20 of the 44 battalions present had fewer than 500 of all ranks. Of the 2nd Battalions present, only one had more than 500 of all ranks, and the remaining eight had an average strength of only 336. Experience, however, could be more important than numbers, as Wellington remarked when it was proposed to replace under-strength 2nd Battalions with stronger 1st Battalions from home:

> 'some of the best and most experienced soldiers in this army, the most healthy and capable of bearing fatigue, are in the 2nd battalions. The 2nd batts. 53rd, 31st, and 66th, for instance, are much more effective, and have always more men for duty in proportion to their gross numbers and fewer sick, than any of the 1st battalions recently arrived.'[5]

The senior infantry corps were the three regiments of Foot Guards (Plates 24–27); in order of seniority the 1st, 2nd or Coldstream and 3rd or Scots Regiments. They served both on campaign and provided the royal bodyguard for ceremonial occasions at home, so the 1st Regiment maintained three battalions and the others two each. Justifiably regarded as an élite, on campaign their battalions were almost always stronger than those of line regiments (at Waterloo, for example, the four Guards battalions were among the seven strongest in the army). Even under the most dire circumstances their

---

4. Anon., *The Battle of Waterloo, containing the Series of Accounts Published by Authority... by a Near Observer*, London 1816, p. xxvii.
5. *The Dispatches of Field Marshal the Duke of Wellington*, ed. J. Gurwood, London 1834–38, Vol. IX, pp. 52–53; entry for 9 April 1812.

conduct was exemplary, as demonstrated perhaps most clearly at the end of the retreat to Corunna when, amid the straggling shambles of the army, the Guards battalions were still marching in order, with their drum major at the head, twirling his mace. It is a testimony to their reputation that Sir John Moore, seeing them at a distance, recognised immediately that 'Those must be the Guards'. The 1st Foot Guards saw service in Flanders 1793–95, in North Holland 1799, in the Mediterranean, the Peninsular War, the Netherlands in 1814, and both 2nd and 3rd Battalions fought at Waterloo. The Coldstream Guards also served in Flanders and North Holland, in Egypt in 1801, Copenhagen in 1807, at Walcheren, in the Peninsula and in the Netherlands in 1814, and the 2nd Battalion at Waterloo. The 3rd or Scots Regiment had a service as extensive as that of the Coldstream, and similarly was represented at Waterloo by its 2nd Battalion.

Most regiments of line infantry were identified by a title as well as by their number. In 1782 it was decided that regiments should bear territorial affiliations, intended to increase *esprit de corps* by associating the regiment with the area from which it drew its recruits. In practice, however, such designations often bore little similarity to the origin of the regiment's personnel, and indeed the county allocation sometimes had no more relevance than being the location of the colonel's estates. Following the authorisation of the enlistment of militiamen, the connection between regimental title and origin of recruits became even more tenuous.

Among the line regiments were three (7th Royal, 21st Royal North British, 23rd Royal Welsh) which bore the title 'Fusiliers' (contemporary spellings included 'Fusileers' and 'Fuzileers'; the last being favoured by the *Army List*; the variations Welsh and Welch also existed for the name of the 23rd). This related to their original armament, in the late 17th century, *fusils* being light muskets; by 1812–15 their distinction was no more than a matter of uniform and *esprit de corps* (Plate 29).

Highland regiments also comprised a small but significant part of the line infantry. In 1809 eleven regiments bore the title 'Highland', but in that year six had their Highland uniform, and in some cases their title, abolished, as it was supposed that the kilt was a hindrance to ordinary recruiting. The regiments which retained Highland dress were the 42nd, 78th, 79th, 92nd and 93rd (Plate 32).

In addition to the light companies of each line regiment, at the period in question six regiments were composed exclusively of light infantry, having been converted from 1803 (those numbered 43rd, 51st, 52nd, 68th, 71st and 85th; plus the 90th, although that regiment was not officially light infantry until 1815). Their specialist training made them expert skirmishers, but unlike the light troops of some armies, they remained equally adept at the more conventional tactics of the ordinary infantry. Sir John Moore was instrumental in the development of light infantry (he was colonel of the 52nd from 1801 until his death at Corunna), but many of the advances he instituted in training had been expressed by earlier exponents of light infantry service. With the assistance of the 52nd's commanding officer, Lieutenant-Colonel Kenneth Mackenzie,[6] Moore made the 52nd a model for the army, and the brigade he trained at Shorncliffe in Kent (with the 43rd and 95th) formed the basis for the Light Division of the army in the Peninsula, arguably the finest formation in the army. Perhaps more important than light infantry tactics was Moore's development of leadership and high morale, founded upon the concept that officers should be trained expertly and should lead and maintain discipline by example, treating their subordinates with every consideration and as humanely as possible. Such theories were entirely vindicated by the outstanding service of the Light Division. (See Plate 33).

Alongside the development of light infantry tactics went experiments with rifled firearms, short-barrelled muskets with 'rifling' inside the barrel which, by imparting a spin upon the projectile, were

6. Later Sir Kenneth Douglas of Glenbervie, the name being adopted on his elevation to a dormant baronetcy in 1830.

capable of much greater accuracy, at enhanced range, than the ordinary smoothbore muskets. Units armed with rifles had been formed in the early French Revolutionary Wars, recruited from foreigners, there being a great tradition of civilian rifle shooting in parts of Germany and Austria. In 1797 it was decided to form a rifle battalion of the regular army, so the 5th Battalion 60th (Royal American) Regiment was created. This regiment, created for service in North America in 1755 and traditionally recruited with foreigners, was the ideal home for men from disbanded 'foreign corps' who already had knowledge of rifle shooting. Rifle companies were added to the 60th's other four battalions, and to the 6th Battalion raised in 1799, but only the 5th Battalion was composed exclusively of riflemen (Plate 34).

To increase the army's 'rifle' capability, in 1800 an 'Experimental Rifle Corps' was assembled with the intention of training men in rifle shooting and then returning them to their units, to form rifle-armed platoons. This policy was changed and a permanent Rifle Corps was established, which in December 1802 was allocated the number 95 in the sequence of line regiments. Under its earliest commanders, notably Coote Manningham (its colonel) and William Stewart, the regiment became an élite formation, arguably the most famous in the army, and expanded with the formation of 2nd and 3rd Battalions in 1805 and 1809 respectively. All three battalions served throughout the Peninsular War, helping the Light Division to achieve its awesome reputation.

Even more than light infantry service, 'rifle' tactics – the ability to skirmish in 'open order', take advantage of natural cover and to target specific individuals within the enemy ranks – required an intelligence and self-reliance far greater than that needed by the ordinary infantrymen who stood in dense formations and fired only at the word of command. The 95th were the skirmishers *par excellence* and the superlative nature of the regiment's officers contributed greatly. Typical was Sir Thomas Sidney Beckwith (1772–1831), an exemplary commanding officer, who served with the 95th in the Peninsula (and commanded a brigade of the Light Division) until he went home, ill, in 1811. A description of his attitude exemplifies the best practice. He was reportedly a man concerned with efficiency in the field rather than parade-ground precision, who gained the trust of his men by kindness:

> '[which was] the surest way to make the soldiers follow him cheerfully through fire and water, when the day of trial came; for they well knew that he was the last man on earth who would give them unnecessary trouble, or, on the other hand, would spare neither man nor officer, when the good of the service demanded their utmost exertions.'[7]

The result was the excellence described in the quotation in the text to Plate 34. The regiment prided itself on having fired the first and last shots in every engagement in which it was present, and this unique record was recognised when, on 16 February 1816, it was removed from the sequence of numbered regiments and given the title 'The Rifle Brigade'.

The distinctive green uniform of the rifle corps, as much as their revolutionary tactics, marked them apart from all the rest of the army; as late as 1861 Sir George Brown (the colonel of the 2nd Battalion) ordered riflemen to take the place of honour at the right of the line, for the appearance of a green-clad unit in the middle of a line of redcoats led him to remark, 'Why, damn me, it looks like a rotten tooth in an old woman's head.'[8]

Plates 24 and 30 illustrate the most precious possessions of every regiment: its Colours. Although these flags were of practical use as a rallying-point in action, they were far more significant than that, by symbolising the regimental identity and honour. No greater disaster or dishonour could befall a regiment than to lose its Colours to the enemy, and so the most bitter combat could rage around their

7. Leach, J., *Rough Sketches of the Life of an Old Soldier*, London 1831, p. 121; reprinted Trotman, London 1986.
8. *Rifle Brigade Chronicle* 1923, p. 183.

possession. Although protection of the Colours was a battalion's most important duty, it was not popular as the Colours always attracted enemy fire: as William Lawrence of the 40th Foot recalled of Waterloo:

'I was ordered to the Colours. This, although I was as used to warfare as much as any, was a job I did not at all like; but still I went as boldly to work as I could. There had been before me that day 14 sergeants already killed and wounded while in charge of these colours, with officers in proportion, and the staff and colours were almost cut to pieces. This job will never be blotted from my memory: although I am now an old man, I remember it as if it had been yesterday. I had not been there more than a quarter of an hour when a cannon-shot took the captain's head clean off.'[9]

The Colours depicted by Hamilton Smith illustrate their large size. By the 1768 Clothing Warrant, which still pertained, they were 6 ft 6 in wide by 6 ft deep, upon a 9 ft 10 in pole, which made then extremely unwieldy, especially when borne by an ensign who might only be a boy. Sir John Moore commented in 1803 that such youths found it almost impossible to keep a Colour upright and steady, while John Cooke, who joined the 43rd Foot a month before his 14th birthday, recalled how he had been blown off his feet when a gust of wind caught the Colour he was carrying. Each battalion had two Colours: a 'King's Colour' of a Union flag with a regimental device in the centre, and a 'Regimental Colour', generally of the regimental facing-colour, with the regimental device and a small Union in the upper canton nearest the pole. In the Foot Guards, each company had a Colour bearing its distinctive badge upon a Union flag, their equivalent of a Regimental Colour, while crimson Colours belonging to the field officers served as their King's Colours.

Plate 36 shows another important part of an infantry battalion: its drummers. They (and buglers in the light infantry) were of great significance in transmitting orders on the battlefield by drum-beat or bugle-call, the only way that instructions could be heard above the cacophony of battle. Regimental bands were also important, their music serving to maintain morale, especially in the midst of battle. In the aftermath of action their members often served as medical orderlies, a practice which still pertains in the British Army. Although officially restricted in size for reasons of expense, many regiments formed larger bands by concealing band members within their ordinary muster-rolls, and many hired professional musicians, including a considerable number of foreigners.

A number of Hamilton Smith's plates depict the infantry's personal equipment, which constituted a formidable burden. Carried on the back by shoulder straps, with a constricting strap across the chest, the knapsack was originally made of unstiffened, painted canvas, but the 'improved' design with a wooden frame, sometimes styled 'Mr Trotter's' after its designer, was even more uncomfortable to carry. John Cooper of the 7th Fusiliers itemised the equipment he carried in the Peninsula: knapsack (3 lb), blanket (4 lb), greatcoat (4 lb), mess-tin (1 lb), dress jacket (3 lb), white undress jacket (½ lb), two shirts and three ruffles (2½ lb), 2 pairs of shoes (3 lb), trousers (2 lb), gaiters (¼ lb), 2 pairs of stockings (1 lb), 2 tent-pegs (½ lb), brushes and comb (3 lb), pipe-clay (1 lb) and, for his duties as a sergeant, pen, ink and paper (¼ lb). Two pipeclayed leather belts (1 lb) supported a leather cartridge-box and 60 rounds of ammunition (6 lb) and a bayonet scabbard; a haversack contained two days' beef (2 lb) and three days' bread (3 lb), and the canteen and belt weighed 4 lb when full. The musket and bayonet weighed 14 lb, bringing the total to 59 lb. Even this was not the maximum: Sergeant-Major Murray of the 3rd Foot Guards estimated that a private of his regiment in the Peninsula in 1812 had to bear a load of 75¾ lb, including the shared burden of carrying a camp-kettle and bill-hook.[10]

9. Lawrence, J., *The Autobiography of Sergeant William Lawrence*, ed. C.N. Bankes, London 1886, p. 210; reprinted as *A Dorset Soldier: The Autobiography of Sgt. William Lawrence, 1790–1869*, ed. E. Hathaway, Spellmount, Tunbridge Wells 1993.
10. Quoted in Colonel W. Knollys' introduction to Lt. Gen. de Fezensac's *A Journal of the Russian Campaign in 1812*, London 1852, p. xlix; reprinted Trotman, Cambridge 1988.

Benjamin Harris of the 95th believed that so great was the weight carried that some men died under it, and so awkwardly was it arranged, 'that the free motion of the body was impeded, the head held down from the pile at the back of the neck, and the soldier half beaten before he came to the scratch.'[11]

It was stated that a greatcoat and blanket (usually carried atop the knapsack) were 'more than [a man] can carry. The Duke of Wellington tried it in the year that his army entered France, but it distressed the troops greatly',[12] and as Cooper noted with feeling, 'the government should have sent us new backbones' to bear the weight.[13]

The musket carried at this time was a smoothbored flintlock known by the generic nickname 'Brown Bess': 'brown' probably from the rustproofing of the barrel, 'Bess' either an alliterative term of endearment or a derivation of the German *Buchse* (gun). The nickname was applied to a number of weapons, from the Short Land Service musket with 42-inch barrel in use at the beginning of the French Wars, to the simplified India Pattern with 39-inch barrel, which became the standard arm of the infantry. There were also light infantry and sergeants' muskets. The weapon was slow to load (three rounds per minute was a good average), unreliable (the mis-fire rate might rise from 15 to 25 per cent in damp weather), and inaccurate; as one experienced officer commented, 'as to firing at a man at 200 yards with a common musket, you may just as well fire at the moon and have the same hope of hitting your object.'[14] Under the prevailing system of tactics, however, it was not necessary for the ordinary musket to be any more accurate. Troops manoeuvred mostly in solid blocks and thus it was only necessary to register a hit anywhere upon a target many yards long, at relatively short range (80–100 yards was probably about the limit of truly effective musketry, and firing often occurred at much closer range). It was because of these circumstances that a well-trained marksman with a superior light infantry musket, or even more a rifle, could be so much more effective than a man with a 'common musket'.

Although much vaunted, the bayonet was used only rarely in combat, except in unusual circumstances or in the storm of fortified places. Bayonet charges were usually only delivered after musketry had disordered the enemy to the extent that they broke before the charge came within bayonet range. The fear of the bayonet, rather than its use, was the decisive factor; in effect, it was the supreme psychological weapon.

The Royal Artillery

The 'technical' services – artillery and engineers – were administered not by the army but by the Board of Ordnance, headed by the Master-General of Ordnance. Five individuals held this post during the French Wars: Charles, 3rd Duke of Richmond 1784–95; Charles, 1st Marquess Cornwallis 1795–1801; John, 2nd Earl of Chatham 1801–06; Francis, 2nd Earl of Moira 1806–07; Chatham again 1807–10; and Henry, 1st Earl of Mulgrave 1810–16.

The Royal Regiment of Artillery comprised three principal branches: the dismounted gunners, sometimes known as the Royal Foot Artillery; the mounted Royal Horse Artillery; and the Corps of Drivers. The main body of Foot Artillery (Plate 39) was organised in battalions of ten companies each; the number of battalions rose to ten in 1808. The battalions never served as units, but each company, with a complement of drivers, formed an autonomous unit, styled a 'brigade' ('battery' is now the more

11. Harris, B.R., *The Recollections of Rifleman Harris*, ed. H. Curling, London 1970 (ed. C. Hibbert), p. 13; reprinted as *A Dorset Rifleman: The Recollections of Benjamin Harris*, ed. E. Hathaway, Shinglepicker Publications, Swanage 1996.
12. 'Militaris', 'On the Equipment of the British Infantry', in *United Service Journal* 1831, Vol. II, p. 204.
13. Cooper, J.S., *Rough Notes of Seven Campaigns in Portugal, Spain, France, and America*, Carlisle 1914, pp. 85–86; reprinted with Introduction by I. Fletcher, Spellmount, Tunbridge Wells 1996.
14. Hanger, G., *To All Sportsmen*, London 1814, p. 205; reprinted as *Colonel George Hanger to all Sportsmen*, Richmond Publishing, Richmond 1971.

usual term, although in contemporary terminology this was used to describe a fixed gun position). Each brigade or company when equipped for field service normally comprised six pieces of ordnance (five cannon and one howitzer) and all supporting vehicles. (Howitzers were the only type of ordnance capable of effective indirect fire, the arching trajectory of their projectiles permitting them to fire over the heads of friendly troops or other obstacles.) The original guns, 6- and 3-pounder cannon, proved much inferior to the opposing French artillery and were replaced by 9-pounders, although not until the Waterloo campaign did these become universal. Similarly, the original howitzers were replaced by the more effective 5½-inch pattern. Companies were usually known by the name of the commanding officer, rather than by a number or other identification.

The concept of light artillery which could accompany cavalry to provide it with immediate fire support originated in the mid-18th century, but not until 1793 was a branch of the Royal Artillery formed for that specific purpose. Like the Foot Artillery, units were composed of six field pieces and their attendant vehicles (a typical establishment is described in the text to Plate 40), and as all combatant personnel of the Royal Horse Artillery either rode on horseback or on the battery vehicles, their rate of movement was very rapid. In 1801 there were seven 'brigades' or troops, rising to twelve by 1806; they were identified either by the name of their commander or by a letter. Some troops retained the 6-pounder cannon throughout the period. At Waterloo, for example, only three troops had 9-pounders, four had light 6-pounders and one (Bull's or 'I' Troop) was equipped exclusively with heavy 5½-inch howitzers.

Compared to the number of guns fielded by some European armies, the British complement was generally small, precluding the establishment of a tactical artillery reserve. In Wellington's field army in the 1812 campaign, for example, there were present only four troops of Royal Horse Artillery, seven brigades of Foot Artillery (one of which maintained the siege train, and another was without guns, serving the ammunition train), and one brigade of King's German Legion Foot Artillery; this meant that no division had more than one brigade or troop of artillery attached to it.

Associated with the Royal Horse Artillery was the Mounted Rocket Corps (see Plate 41), and the Royal Artillery's Corps of Drivers which is covered in the text to Plate 42.

Engineers and Transport

As a result of the experience of the Peninsular War, the engineer service received a greater overhaul than any other part of the army. At the beginning of the war it comprised the Corps of Royal Engineers, and the Royal Military Artificers.

The Royal Engineers was a unit composed exclusively of officers, all highly trained but with a comparatively high proportion of elderly members, so that the more active ones were terribly over-worked. Of 102 who served in the Peninsula, 24 were killed in action and one died of exhaustion, and their casualty rate was such that Wellington once remarked that, although they were so needed, he hardly dare request more engineer officers lest they too became casualties. To supplement them, many line officers with elementary engineering training were seconded as 'assistant engineers'.

Initially, the Royal Military Artificers provided the engineer 'other ranks'. The unit comprised twelve companies of artisans, each commanded by a sub-lieutenant, who were stationed in fortresses to act as carpenters and builders. Only the most expendable were sent on campaign. In November 1809, for example, the entire complement with the Peninsular army was two sergeants and 23 other ranks, of whom two were missing and four ill. As late as the siege of Burgos only eight men could be mustered. Consequently, all the manual work had to be undertaken by untrained infantrymen, acting as labourers.

William Napier's condemnation was entirely justified:

'To the discredit of the English government, no army was ever so ill provided [with engineers]... The engineer officers were exceedingly zealous... but the ablest trembled when reflecting upon their utter destitution of all that belonged to real service... the best officers and the finest soldiers were obliged to sacrifice themselves in a lamentable manner... The sieges carried on in Spain were a succession of butcheries, because the commonest resources of their art were denied to the engineers.'[15]

Finally, following the carnage of the second siege of Badajoz (where 13 of the 19 engineer officers present became casualties), the government heeded Wellington's demand for trained engineers, and in April 1812 the Royal Military Artificers or Sappers and Miners was formed (titled as just the Royal Sappers and Miners from 1813), with an establishment of 2,800 rank and file trained in engineering at Chatham, organised in regular companies, and commanded by engineer officers. For the 1813 campaign in the Peninsula some 300 were present, and from San Sebastian onwards they made a considerable difference to the conduct of sieges. Both they and the Royal Engineers are illustrated in Plate 43; and another engineer unit, the Royal Staff Corps, is described in the text to Plate 4.

In terms of size, when compared to the enormity of the task, the army's transport service was one of the least efficient branches. Throughout the period, much of the transportation of military supplies was dependent upon civilian contractors who supplied both vehicles and personnel, perhaps most famously the mule-trains and ox-carts used in the Peninsula. The imperfections of the service are exemplified by Wellington's complaint regarding the delay in investing Ciudad Rodrigo:

'We must expect disappointments when we have to deal with Portuguese and Spanish carters and muleteers... What do you think of empty carts taking two days to go ten miles on a good road? After all, I am obliged to appear satisfied, or they would all desert!'[16]

A remedy was attempted by the formation of an army transport service in 1794, the Corps of Royal Waggoners, but with its personnel selected from men declared unfit for field service, not much could be expected, and it failed completely. A second attempt was made in August 1799 when a new Royal Waggon Train was formed, originally of five troops, increasing to 14 troops by 1814, details of which are given in the text to Plate 45.

The Foreign Regiments

A considerable proportion of the British Army was composed of 'foreign corps', units whose personnel were drawn from overseas. Large numbers of foreign or émigré corps had been enrolled during the period of the French Revolutionary Wars, but although most of these were disbanded before or at the time of the Peace of Amiens, as late as 1813 about one in eight of the men of the regular army was of foreign origin, and although numbers were found in British regiments, most were concentrated into specifically 'foreign' units.

As part of the regular British Army, the West Indian regiments were not 'foreign' *per se*, but as only their officers were of British origin, they may be considered here (Plate 46).

British possessions in the West Indies were relatively small in area but extremely important

15. Napier, W.F.P., *History of the War in the Peninsula and South of France*, London 1832–40, Vol. III, pp. 525–26.
16. *The Dispatches of Field Marshal the Duke of Wellington*, ed. J. Gurwood, London 1834–38, Vol. VIII, p. 514; entry for 7 January 1812.

commercially, as the source of sugar, spices and other commodities. Considerable military and naval resources were expended during the French Revolutionary and Napoleonic Wars to secure British possessions in the Caribbean, and to capture others. Such operations included not only successful conquests but futile expeditions like that to San Domingo, and the suppression of internal unrest like the 'Maroon revolt' in Jamaica. These cost many casualties, but much greater causes of death and incapacitation were the climate and diseases of the region, more lethal than any number of pitched battles. For example, in the Leeward and Windward Islands between 1796 and 1805, 24,916 troops died, and countless more were invalided with ruined health; in bad years more than one-third of the garrison of those territories died (in 1796 6,585 men were lost, 41.3 per cent of the troops stationed there). These statistics were not exceptional. For example, the average loss of troops in Jamaica and Honduras between 1810 and 1828 was 15.5 per cent.[17]

To reduce the loss of troops from Britain, local regiments were formed, recruited either from those already resident in the region, or from African slaves, purchased for the purpose by the government, prior to the abolition of the slave trade in 1807. They were found to be very much more resistant to the diseases and climate of the region than were European troops, and despite the vile way in which recruits were obtained (slavery), they proved to be good troops. One notable exception was the mutiny of the 8th West India Regiment at Dominica in April 1802, which was suppressed by force, although this outbreak was evidently not unconnected to the character and career of the regimental colonel, Andrew Cochrane-Johnstone, an outright rogue whose governorship of that island was marked by tyranny and corruption.

The first West Indian corps were small independent units like Malcolm's Royal Rangers, formed by Lieutenant Robert Malcolm of the 41st Foot in Martinique in 1794. In 1795 orders were issued for the formation of eight regiments of foot, known originally by the names of their colonels, and numbered as West India Regiments from 1798. One of these was disbanded in 1796, but five more were authorised in 1798, taking the number to twelve. Between 1802 and 1804 the 9th–12th Regiments were disbanded, with the 8th being re-constituted from the old 11th, following the Dominica mutiny.

The largest and most notable of the 'foreign corps', and among the best troops in the entire army, was the King's German Legion (Plate 47). In one sense the KGL was less 'foreign' than other units of non-British origin, in that it was formed originally from subjects of King George III, albeit from his Hanoverian territories. Hanoverian troops fought alongside the British in a number of campaigns in the 18th century, but in June 1803 Hanover was over-run by the French. Authority was given for the British Army to recruit those of the King's Hanoverian subjects who wished to continue the fight against Napoleon, to form a unit styled 'the King's Germans', but when energetic recruiting produced a considerable exodus, the force was expanded to form what was in effect a self-contained miniature army, containing all arms of service, which required the change of title to the King's German Legion. The establishment expanded progressively and finally included eight line infantry battalions, two of light infantry, five regiments of cavalry, plus horse and foot artillery, and a small corps of engineer officers. The Legion served in the Peninsula, in the Mediterranean, Walcheren, North Germany 1813–14 and the Waterloo campaign, and throughout maintained the highest standards. Indeed, it was acknowledged in the Peninsula that at least some of the Legion cavalry was superior to the British, notably in their expertise in 'outpost' duty and reconnaissance, elements of cavalry service not much practised in the British Army and which had to be learned on campaign.

It became increasingly difficult to obtain German recruits of the calibre of the originals, so other

17. Marshall, H., 'Contributions to Statistics of the British Army', *Edinburgh Medical and Surgical Journal*, July 1835.

nationalities were accepted into the Legion, including even deserters and ex-prisoners-of-war, but if this led to a slight decline in the overall standard of private soldier, the calibre of the Legion remained high throughout, probably due to the high quality of officers and NCOs. The former included a limited number of British, although the majority were of German origin. Although nationality is not always obvious from the name, in July 1815 some ten per cent of the Legion officers bore British names, less than four per cent French or Italian, and the remainder German. In all some 28,000 men served in the Legion between its creation and its disbandment at the end of the Napoleonic Wars, with a peak strength in excess of 14,000 in mid-1812; in 1814 the non-Hanoverians were discharged, so that for the Waterloo campaign its units were considerably reduced in strength.

The units of the Legion were dressed very much as the respective branches of the regular British Army; details for the infantry are given in the text to Plate 47; facings are illustrated in Plate 51.

The five regiments of German Legion cavalry initially comprised two of dragoons and three of light dragoons. The dragoons – who originally wore red heavy cavalry uniform with blue facings and gold lace – were converted to the 1st and 2nd Light Dragoons of the Legion on 25 December 1813, at which date the existing 1st–3rd Light Dragoons were re-titled as the 1st–3rd Hussars, although they had been known unofficially as hussars before that date. The new 1st and 2nd Light Dragoons wore the 1812 light dragoon uniform (see text to Plates 14 and 16) with red facings and gold and silver lace respectively. The new 1st–3rd Hussars had worn hussar dress before they were officially titled as such, with red facings and gold lace, white facings and gold lace, and yellow facings and silver lace, for the 1st–3rd Regiments respectively. They wore fur caps – Beamish's history[18] shows busbies with peaks for the 2rd and 3rd – but Hamilton Smith shows a light dragoon-style shako of the type adopted by other British hussar regiments for use on campaign, as described in the text to Plate 47.

The 1st Hussars served throughout the Peninsular War, and were joined there by the 2nd Hussars in April 1811. The services of the 3rd Hussars are described in the text to Plate 47.

Another German formation was the so-called 'Brunswick Oels Corps', alias the 'Black Legion' (see Plate 50). The ruling family of Brunswick had close connections with the British royal family, so it was appropriate that for some years Brunswick troops were part of the British Army's 'foreign corps'. One Duke of Brunswick-Oels, Karl Wilhelm Ferdinand (1735–1806) was brother-in-law to King George III by virtue of his marriage to George's sister Augusta (1737–1813), and as a Prussian field marshal opposed the French in 1792. He was still fighting them when he was mortally wounded at Auerstädt. He was succeeded by his son, Duke Friedrich Wilhelm (1771–1815), George III's nephew, whose lands were seized by Napoleon. An implacable opponent of the French, he was regarded as a model patriot by the anti-French camp, and in 1809 formed the Brunswick Legion for Austrian service to continue the fight. Following the defeat of Austria, he marched into Westphalia, and when no substantial anti-French rising materialised, he fought his way to the coast and was evacuated by a British fleet. The Brunswick Corps then entered British service, and fought in the Peninsula, as described in the text to Plate 50. After Napoleon's abdication the Brunswick Corps formed the nucleus of a new national army, which fought alongside the British in the Waterloo campaign, and it was at their head that the Duke was killed at Quatre Bras.

Other foreign corps are included in the relevant charts (Plates 38 and 51). These plates are described here.

A number of units are shown in the charts which were associated with various overseas colonies. Three 'condemned' or penal corps are included in Plate 38. **The Royal African Corps** was formed in

18. Beamish, L., *History of the King's German Legion*, Hanover 1832; reprinted Buckland & Brown, London 1993.

August 1800 and received that title in 1804; like the others it was a receptacle for deserters, criminals, and the worst of the turncoat prisoners-of-war, their service in the most hostile or unhealthy environments being a scarcely more lenient alternative to imprisonment. In October 1806 part was detached to form the **Royal West India Rangers**, and in August 1807 the African contingent was re-named the **Royal York Rangers**. Half was stationed in West Africa and half in Guernsey, the latter proceeding to the West Indies in September 1808 and keeping the new name, while the African part reverted to the title of Royal African Corps. In May 1810 the regiment was authorised to enlist Africans; in 1817 six companies of Europeans were sent to the Cape and were disbanded there in 1821, the remainder having been disbanded in 1819. The Royal West India Rangers served at Guadeloupe in 1815 and was disbanded in June 1819; the Royal York Rangers served at Martinique and Guadeloupe (1810 and 1815) and was also disbanded in June 1819.

The four **Ceylon Regiments** (shown in Plate 38) originated when the existing Malay Regiment (initially part of the Dutch garrison which entered the service of the East India Company when the island was occupied by the British) transferred to the King's service in 1801. With the formation of another battalion, they became the 1st and 2nd Ceylon Regiments; the 3rd was formed in 1803, and after the purchase of slaves was authorised, a 4th Regiment was created, entirely African in composition. In 1814 the 1st was converted to light infantry, and was Malay and Javanese in composition; the 2nd was largely Malay and Sinhalese, and the 3rd and 4th African. The two latter were disbanded in 1817 and 1815 respectively, and the 2nd in 1821. The 1st remained in existence until 1874.

The **Cape Regiment** (Plate 38) was formed in 1806, largely from members of the captured Cape garrison who had not already entered British service in the 60th Foot, and from Hottentots. It remained to garrison the Cape until disbanded in September 1817. The **Bourbon Regiment** (Plate 38) was formed from the captured garrison of that island (Réunion) in January 1812, and remained there until disbanded in 1816. **The Royal Foreign Artillery** (Plate 38) was formed from existing corps of émigré gunners in 1802, and served in the West Indies until disbanded in 1817.

De Meuron's Regiment (Plate 51) was originally Swiss, transferring from Dutch to British service after the capture of Ceylon in 1795. After service in India, it served in the Mediterranean, and subsequently in the War of 1812; one of the best foreign regiments, it was disbanded in July 1816. **De Roll's Regiment** (Plate 51) was also Swiss, formed in 1794, and distinguished in Egypt in 1801. A detachment served in eastern Spain in 1813 while the rest of the regiment was in the Mediterranean; it was disbanded in 1816. **Dillon's Regiment** (Plate 51) originated in 1795, its recruits originally French, German and Italian. It also served with distinction in Egypt in 1801, and a detachment served in eastern Spain in 1813; it was disbanded in 1814. **Watteville's Regiment** (Plate 51) was also largely Swiss, formed in 1801, served well in Egypt later that year, and was subsequently in the Mediterranean (including at Maida). In 1813 it was sent to Canada for the War of 1812, and was disbanded in 1816.

The **Chasseurs Britanniques** (Plate 51) was formed in 1801, originally from French émigrés but subsequently was diluted in quality by the enlistment of ex-prisoners-of-war and other nationalities, including Italians and eastern Europeans. It served with some distinction in the Peninsular War – notably at Fuentes de Oñoro – but its desertion record was such that it was not trusted with 'outpost' duty. It was disbanded in August 1814. **The Royal Corsican Rangers** (Plate 51) was authorised in September 1803, and raised by Hudson Lowe (1769–1844), later famous as Napoleon's 'gaoler' at St Helena. One of the better foreign corps, it served in the Mediterranean, was constituted as a rifle or light infantry corps and wore a uniform based upon that of the 5th Battalion 60th. It was disbanded at Corfu in 1816.

The **Sicilian Regiment** (Plate 51) was a light infantry corps raised in 1806 by Sir John Stuart when he was in command of the British forces in southern Italy. Composed of Sicilians, it served its entire existence in the Mediterranean (including the Egyptian expedition of 1807) and was disbanded in 1816.

The **York Chasseurs** (Plate 51) was another 'condemned' or penal corps, raised for West Indian service in 1813; it served at Guadeloupe (1815) and was disbanded in August 1819.

The **French Independent Companies** (Plate 51) were formed with a strength of two companies in 1812 from French prisoners-of-war and were intended for garrison duty in the West Indies. About the worst of the foreign corps, they behaved with disgraceful indiscipline in the expedition to Hampton, Virginia, in June 1813, plundering and murdering, and were disbanded in May 1814. The unit styled Foreign Veterans (Plate 51) was actually the **1st Foreign Veteran Battalion**, or the Veteran Battalion of the King's German Legion. It was authorised in December 1812 for men of the KGL who were not fit for proper active service, and was disbanded in 1816.

In 1808 the New South Wales Corps was taken into the line as the 102nd Foot, and when that regiment was under orders to return to Britain, those men who were anxious to remain in New South Wales, by having families settled there, were permitted to leave the 102nd. In March 1810 the governor of the colony (the commander of the new garrison unit, the 1st Battalion 73rd Foot, Lieutenant-Colonel Lachlan Macquarie) formed the **Veteran Company, New South Wales** (Plate 51), to accommodate them. It was ordered to be attached to the regular garrison unit, and was disbanded in 1823.

Two foreign corps not shown in the charts, but which have been added by hand to one recorded example of the plate, were the **Calabrian Free Corps** and the **Anglo-Italian Levy**. The former, titled 'Calabrese Corps: 1 regt.' in the chart, was raised in Sicily from Calabrian rebels in 1809, served in the Mediterranean, in eastern Spain 1813–14 and at Genoa in 1814. The chart shows the uniform as dark blue with yellow facings, white lace (silver for officers) and green breeches. The Anglo-Italian Levy, described in the chart as 'Italian Levy: 4 regts.', formed partially from ex-prisoners-of-war and other elements, served in eastern Spain and in the Mediterranean. The chart indicates dark blue uniform with red facings, white lace (silver for officers) and grey breeches.

The Militia

The militia was the statutory home-defence force, comprising infantry battalions raised by each county, by a mixture of voluntary recruitment and by ballot among the citizens of the county. This last was the only form of conscription prevailing at the time, but it was selective, in that not all of society was included in the ballot, and service was not compulsory: a man chosen by the ballot could provide a substitute to serve in his place if he (or his employer) could afford to pay for one. In practice, many more substitutes served than did ballotted men. The militia regiments were embodied in time of war for full-time service, but could not be sent out of their country of origin without their own consent. Apart from relieving the regular army of home-defence duties, at the period in question the militia provided a most valuable source of recruits for the regular army. After the legalisation of the transfer of men from the militia to the regulars (a process entirely voluntary), the regulars gained a steady stream of recruits already trained in the use of arms and used to military discipline, so that much of the improvement in the army at the time of the Peninsular War may be ascribed to this influx of high-quality recruits.

Plate 52 lists the regiments of county militia, arranged by the numbers 1–71 in the English, Welsh and Scottish list, covering 91 units. The numbering was that of the 'precedence list' of the militia organisation. In the mid-18th century the question of seniority had caused some jealousy among militia regiments, so from 1760 it was ordered that any regiments which happened to be serving together should draw lots to determine which would be senior and which junior among them. This system was not satisfactory, so for the next major embodiment of the militia (1778), a precedence number was drawn by ballot for each regiment, and the ballot was redrawn every year (so that, for example, militia regiment no. 1 was Southampton (Hampshire) in 1778, West Yorkshire in 1779, Essex in 1780, East Yorkshire in 1781 and Oxfordshire in 1782). This, too, was found to be unsatisfactory, so that upon the next embodiment the numbers drawn lasted until 1803, and those drawn upon the renewal of the war in 1803 remained unchanged until 1833. It is the last system (1803–33) that is shown in Plate 52. Where a county maintained more than one militia battalion, both shared the same precedence number (e.g. the three Middlesex battalions – East, West and Westminster – all occupied the number 20). However, since the three Ridings of Yorkshire were separate administrative regions, their regiments (East, North and West) were allocated separate numbers.

The Scottish militia was not embodied until 1797 and initially had its own precedence list, which was only integrated with that of the English and Welsh regiments in 1803. Only abbreviated titles are given in the chart: for example, the Inverness, Banff, Elgin and Nairn Militia appears just as 'Inverness'. Full titles are given in Appendix 2, page 174. Details of the Irish Militia are in the text to Plate 52.

Plate 51 includes the three **Provisional Battalions of Militia** which were formed from volunteers from a number of militia regiments for service in the Peninsular War. They arrived there just too late to participate in any of the fighting. The 1st Battalion was commanded by the Marquess of Buckingham, whose own Buckinghamshire Militia provided almost half its personnel, with others from the 1st and 2nd Royal Surrey, Cambridge, Northampton and Worcester Militias. The 2nd Battalion was commanded by Lieutenant-Colonel Edward Bayly of the West Middlesex Militia, whose regiment formed almost half the battalion, with others from the Leicester, Wiltshire, Sussex and East Suffolk Militia. The 3rd Battalion was led by Sir Watkin Williams Wynn Bt. of the Denbighshire Militia, much of the battalion being drawn from the 2nd West York Militia (along with the Denbigh, Hereford, Westmoreland and Derby Militias). Wynn was given the command because 135 of his own Denbigh men only agreed to go if he were their leader. The whole formed a brigade under Major-General Sir Henry Bayly (Edward Bayly's brother), and although their appearance was complimented once they had arrived in the south of France, Rees Gronow, an officer of the Foot Guards, thought them 'a sorry sight' when compared with the hardened veterans of the Peninsular army, and he complained that they were too susceptible to indulgence in cheap French wine and brandy.[19] As each militia regiment had its own facing colour and lace, new uniforms had to be issued for the Provisional Battalions, with blue facings and white lace.

The Royal Marines

Although not part of the Army, Plate 53 depicts the Corps of Royal Marines, the military force controlled by the Admiralty. Its ancestry dates from 1664, but its lineage was not unbroken, and not until 1755 were companies of marines established permanently. Organised originally in three 'Divisions' (Chatham, Portsmouth and Plymouth; a 4th Division was formed at Woolwich in 1805), the force was subdivided into companies, but these were largely administrative units. In practice, personnel were allocated as required among the ships of the fleet, roughly at a rate of one marine per gun, so that a 1st-rate ship-

19. Gronow, R.H., *The Reminiscences and Recollections of Captain Gronow*, London 1964, pp. 333–34.

of-the-line of 100 guns might have about 100 marines, plus a captain and three subalterns (out of a total ship's complement of roughly 950 men), while at the other end of the scale, an 18-gun sloop might have 18 marines with a sergeant in command. Between 1808 and 1814 the regulated strength of the Corps of Royal Marines was no less than 31,400 men.

Trained and organised as infantry, they were versatile, able to fight on land in the numerous amphibious operations and raids conducted throughout the period, and at sea were able to help man the ships' guns and to serve as marksmen and in boarding parties in sea battles. A subsidiary duty was to discourage mutiny among the seamen; aboard ship their quarters were between those of the officers and the seamen. Their value was recognised by the grant of the title 'Royal Marines' on 29 April 1802. Earl St Vincent, who was instrumental in the securing of that award, remarked that it was little enough, for he had never known a circumstance in which the marines had not exceeded everything required of them in loyalty, courage and honour. They were, he stated, the country's sheet-anchor in time of danger.

The East India Company's Army

Although the forces of the Honourable East India Company were essentially a private army, maintained by the company, they were integrated completely with the 'King's regiments' which served in India for the purposes of campaign, and as such were included by Hamilton Smith in his plates (Plates 57–60). The company and its forces were organised in three 'Presidencies', of Madras, Bombay and Bengal, each maintaining its own army. These included units of European infantry and artillery, but the vast proportion were 'Native' regiments of cavalry and infantry, composed of Indian personnel with European officers.

Senior of the company's forces were the European infantry regiments, details of which are given in the text to Plate 60. Originating in 1756, the six battalions of Bengal European Infantry had been reduced to three in 1796, and further reductions in 1798 and 1803 left just the one illustrated in Plate 60. European infantry in Madras dated from the early British settlement, a regiment being constituted in 1748 and increasing to six regiments, but these were reduced to two in 1796 and to one in 1799. The Bombay European Infantry was formed in 1668 from independent companies founded in 1662; increased to two regiments in 1788, it reverted to a single battalion in 1796.

All three presidencies maintained artillery units, established in 1748. They were principally European in composition but included some Indian *Golundauze* (personnel who assisted the European gunners). Their uniforms were generally based upon those of the Royal Artillery, blue with red facings and yellow lace. The élite of the artillery were the horse batteries. In Bengal the first was formed in 1800 but it was only made permanent in 1809, numbering three troops. The Madras Horse Artillery was formed in April 1805 and increased to two troops in 1809; the first Bombay troop was formed in 1811, although it does not appear separately in the chart. Their uniform was based upon the British model, and evidently the Tarleton light dragoon helmet was used at this time.

Although rightly regarded as an élite, the company's European troops were not immune from the temptations which beset most soldiers at the time. As one officer remarked, pointing to a mountain:

> 'Do you see that peak? Place a Bengal artilleryman alone on the top of that peak in the morning, and he'll be drunk before night, wherever it may come from! Upon my soul, I think they could get liquor out of the rock itself!'[20]

20. Bancroft, N.W., *From Recruit to Staff Sergeant*, Simla 1900, pp. 37–38; reprinted with Introduction by B.P. Hughes, Ian Henry Publications, Hornchurch 1979.

All three presidencies maintained a corps of engineers, composed exclusively of officers. The Bengal Engineers had worn blue with scarlet facings, but in December 1806 this was altered to the blue with black velvet facings shown in Plate 60. The Madras Engineers had worn blue with black velvet facings as early as an order of December 1794, colouring which remained unchanged until the adoption of scarlet with purple facings, ordered in December 1818. In Bombay the engineers seem to have worn artillery uniform, until in December 1800 they were ordered to adopt black velvet facings. There were also units of 'other rank' engineers: in Bengal a corps of Pioneers was formed in 1803, which from December 1809 was ordered to wear green with green facings, yellow lace and black buttons. In Madras, a Pioneer Corps formed in 1780 was enlarged until it became two battalions in 1803, evidently wearing dark green with black facings as shown by Hamilton Smith, colouring confirmed in 1823. The same colouring was worn by the corps of Bombay Pioneers authorised in 1777.

The Bengal Native Cavalry had a chequered existence in the 18th century, with a number of creations and reductions. The 1st Regiment originated in 1777 and the 2nd in 1778, the 3rd was formed in 1796, the 4th in 1797, the 5th and 6th in 1800 and the 7th and 8th in 1806. Details of their uniforms are given in the text to Plate 57. Bengal also had units of 'irregular' or 'Local Horse': Skinner's Horse (raised 1803, with 2nd and 3rd Regiments formed 1814 and 1815), Gardner's Horse (1809), and three regiments of Rohilla Cavalry. Although the British officers of these irregular units wore light dragoon uniform, the other ranks were permitted to wear local styles of dress, albeit in 'uniform' colouring, and even Indian metal helmets.

Although a number of units had existed earlier, not until 1784 was a regular body of Native Cavalry formed in Madras. The number of regiments rose to seven in 1800 and eight in 1804. As shown in Plate 60, their uniforms were red with facings of 'Saxon blue' for the 1st Regiment (changed to white in March 1811), and for Regiments 2–8 respectively were dark green, buff, deep yellow, black, French grey, bright yellow and pale yellow. This colouring changed shortly before the chart was published: it was ordered in February 1813 that from January 1814 the Madras Cavalry would wear blue, with facings pale yellow (1st and 5th), orange (2nd and 6th), buff (3rd and 7th), and deep yellow (4th and 8th).

Until 1816 the Bombay Presidency maintained only a single troop of cavalry, formed in 1803 and apparently dressed in red.

The first units of regular infantry were raised in the Bengal Presidency in 1757, the strength increasing until 36 battalions existed by 1785. (See Plate 59). Reorganisation in 1796 reduced the number of regiments to twelve, each of two battalions, but more were raised until there were 27 regiments by 1804, which are those shown in Plate 60. Three more (28th–30th) were formed in 1815.

The first battalions of Madras Native Infantry were formed in 1758, and a reorganisation of 1796 reduced the number of independent units by linking pairs of battalions. By 1807 the number of regiments had risen to 25, although the 1st and 23rd had been disbanded in 1806 after the mutiny at Vellore. (See Plates 58 and 60).

The Bombay Presidency maintained infantry units from 1662, but battalion organisation originated only in 1768. As with the other presidencies, there was considerable reorganisation, until by 1796 there were thirteen battalions. In that year the infantry was reorganised into five regiments of two battalions each; by 1800 there were eight regiments, and the 9th was formed in 1803 (the 1st Battalion from the Bombay Fencibles, a corps formed in 1799 and disbanded in 1806). (See Plate 60.)

The Uniforms of 1812–15

Hamilton Smith's *Costume of the Army* depicts the uniforms 'according to the Last Regulations'; but the changes introduced in 1811–12 were not universal, and there was no single, new clothing regulation which applied to every part of the army. Neither were the changes instituted implemented immediately, so elements of the previous uniforms were retained for some time, and even worn in combination with new items. The most profound of the alterations affected the cavalry, and to a lesser extent the infantry.

Prior to these alterations, the British Army had worn a very distinctive set of uniforms, which were easily recognisable at a distance, a factor which involved more than the predominantly red uniform colour of the infantry and heavy cavalry. It was this practical aspect of uniform design that was Wellington's only concern, not the minutiae; as William Grattan remarked of the army in the Peninsula:

> 'Lord Wellington was a most indulgent commander… provided we brought our men into the field
> well appointed, and with sixty rounds of good ammunition each, he never looked to see whether
> their trousers were black, blue or grey; and as to ourselves, we might be rigged out in all the colours
> of the rainbow if we fancied it.'[1]

Wellington's own comments on the subject were made to Henry Torrens (Military Secretary to the Commander-in-Chief) in November 1811, when Wellington had received information about the proposed uniform changes. He quoted the case of Captain Benjamin Lutyens of the 11th Light Dragoons who had been captured near Elvas by mistaking French troops for the 3rd Hussars of the King's German Legion:

> 'I hear that measures are in contemplation to alter the clothing, caps, &c., of the army.
>
> There is no subject of which I understand so little; and, abstractedly speaking, I think it indifferent
> how a soldier is clothed, provided it is in a uniform manner; and that he is forced to keep himself
> clean and smart, as a soldier ought to be. But there is one thing I deprecate, and that is any imitation
> of the French, in any manner.
>
> It is impossible to form an idea of the inconvenience and injury which result from having any thing
> like them, either on horseback or on foot. Lutyens and his piquet were taken in June because the
> 3rd Hussars had the same caps as the French *Chasseurs à Cheval* and some of their hussars; and I
> was near being taken on the 25th September from the same cause.

---

1. Grattan, W., *Adventures with the Connaught Rangers*, ed. Sir Charles Oman, London 1902, p. 50; reprinted by Greenhill Books, London 1989.

At a distance, or in an action, colors [sic] are nothing: the profile, and shape of the man's cap, and his general appearance, are what guide us; and why should we make our people look like the French? A *cock-tailed* horse is a good mark for a dragoon, if you can get a side view of him; but there is no such mark as the English helmet, and, as far as I can judge, it is the best cover a dragoon can have for his head.

I mention this, because in all probability you may have something to say on these alterations; and I only beg that *we* may be as different as possible from the French in every thing.

The narrow top caps of our infantry, as opposed to their broad top caps, are a great advantage to those who are to look at long lines of posts opposed to each other.'[2]

Wellington's advice went largely unheeded by those authorities at home who were determined to introduce new styles of uniform, and the appearance of the cavalry in particular was altered radically. Details of the uniforms are given in the text to individual plates, but some comments are also necessary here.

The heavy cavalry had worn red jackets with bars of lace across the breast, and either cocked hats or cylindrical 'watering caps', a form of shako. These were replaced by single-breasted jackets closed on the breast by hooks and eyes, with lace vertically down the opening instead of the previous horizontal bars; but the most profound change was to introduce a combed helmet with a crest, as illustrated in Plates 9 and 11. Its use, however, was of brief duration; probably only limited numbers were issued, and when found to be 'in every way objectionable' they were replaced, very quickly, by a second pattern of helmet, as shown in the background of Plate 2. This had a leather skull with brass fittings, including a front-plate which bore a crowned, reversed 'GR' cypher over an oval plaque bearing the identity of the regiment, and a brass comb which supported a horsehair aigrette at the front, and a falling mane at the rear. Unlike the original helmet, it had no plume.

It was this helmet that was worn at Waterloo by three of the four heavy regiments of line cavalry present (1st Dragoon Guards, 1st and 6th Dragoons; the 2nd Dragoons retained their traditional bearskin caps, as shown in Plate 10). Subsequently Hamilton Smith produced amended versions of both Plates 9 and 11, showing the maned helmet instead of the original version. As with all the new uniform changes, the date at which they actually came into use seems to have varied considerably. For example, portraits exist of officers of the 1st Dragoon Guards wearing the 1812 jacket and the original pattern of helmet, or conversely the second pattern (maned) helmet and sabretache (also introduced in August 1812), in conjunction with the previous pattern of jacket.[3]

Despite the resemblance of the helmet to that worn by French dragoons, it was not unpopular with some who wore it, perhaps because the previous cocked hats were prone to warp out of shape. Captain Ralph Heathcote of the Royal Dragoons, for example, wrote in April 1813 that the new helmets were a change 'altogether better than otherwise',[4] although another bewailed the fact that, 'The Queen's Bays, who had one of the handsomest uniforms in any service, are now a sort of modern antique without a similarity, unless, indeed, in the older wardrobes of the theatres.'[5]

The new light dragoon uniform (Plates 14, 16, 17 and 20) was another matter. Instead of the previous braided, waist-length jacket and fur-crested Tarleton helmet, a plastron-fronted, Polish-style, short-tailed jacket and a French-style shako were introduced. Despite the handsome nature of the Tarleton (which was retained by the Horse Artillery: see Plates 40–42), it had not been popular

2. *The Dispatches of Field Marshal the Duke of Wellington*, ed. J. Gurwood, London 1834–38, Vol. VIII, pp. 371–72.

3. See Sumner, Revd. P., 'An Officer of the 1st Dragoon Guards', in *Journal of the Society for Army Historical Research*, Vol. XXII (1943), p. 35.

4. Heathcote, R., *From Ralph Heathcote: Letters of a Young Diplomatist and Soldier during the time of Napoleon*, ed. Countess G. Groben, London 1907.

5. *Royal Military Chronicle*, January 1813, p. 210.

universally. For example, William Tomkinson of the 16th Light Dragoons complained in 1810 that they became:

'so warped by the sun that the men could scarcely wear them. They are bad things for a soldier, only looking well for a few months; the first rain puts them out of shape. All the silver to the edging comes off with both officers and men, and the sooner we adopt some other head-dress the better.'[6]

Nevertheless, the new uniform was so French in style that it appalled many observers. One officer described how, being used to minor changes in uniform:

'I expected to see something on returning home; but certainly not to see anything so extraordinary as part of our cavalry, who are absolutely metamorphosed, in external appearance, to Frenchmen. On crossing the parade at the Horse Guards, I observed several nondescripts, and, on questioning a serjeant, was told, to my utter astonishment, that they were Englishmen and soldiers, belonging to the 13th Light Dragoons!! I could not avoid observing it was fortunate that they were in a country where the prejudice against French Uniforms is not so prevalent as in Spain or Portugal, otherwise those gentlemen would require an efficient guard to protect them from the natives, who, in spite of their talking English fluently, would believe them to be nothing but *Daimoneos de Franceses* [French devils] and shiver them accordingly. Had I not come from a country where they know better, I should have concluded that the British army had been so completely disgraced, that it was found expedient to alter the form and contexture of the army so essentially, that it might be entirely forgotten what it had been, in the hopes of what it might become... I presume they had been altered and altered till no English alteration remained, and it was therefore necessary to adopt French ones... I sincerely hope I shall never live to see the day that it will be necessary to model the British army on that of the French before we can beat them. I do not say that we may not improve from an enemy, but copying the French in a general way is like "Rome learning arts from Greece, whom she had subdued".'[7]

Another officer recorded seeing 'the New Light Dragoon Dress; everyone agreed that it was quite shocking.'[8] Another complaint was the expense to which officers would be put. Berkeley Paget, brother of the Marquess of Anglesey and himself an officer of the 7th Light Dragoons in the Peninsula,[9] recorded how an officer of the 23rd Light Dragoons claimed that it would cost about £300 each to be entirely re-uniformed. (When one of his men was dressed in the new pattern he was greeted by his fellows with cries of, 'Who's that damned Frenchman?')

General Robert Long, on seeing some 9th Light Dragoons arrived from England, wrote in February 1812:

'We have been favored [sic] (not gratified) with a sight of the new projected dress for the Dragoons, and I confess I was not a little disgusted by the spectacle. To see the British Army denationalised as it were in appearance to pay a compliment to French taste, is what my English blood cannot brook... The Tyrant will still continue to hate us, and despise the mind that prefers the livery of the monkey to the leopard's skin.'[10]

By January 1813, presumably referring to his own brigade (9th and 13th Light Dragoons), Long noted that the new uniforms had been issued, a 'sad and vicious taste' which made them impossible to distinguish from the French at any distance, and which could lead them to be killed by the Spanish who

6. Tomkinson, W., *The Diary of a Cavalry Officer in the Peninsula and Waterloo Campaign*, ed. J. Tomkinson, London 1895, p. 40; reprinted with Introduction by the Marquess of Anglesey, Spellmount, Staplehurst 1999.
7. *Royal Military Chronicle*, January 1813, pp. 209–11.
8. Barrett, C.R.B., *History of the XIII Hussars*, Edinburgh 1911, Vol. II, p. 265.
9. See Hylton, Lord, *The Paget Brothers, 1790–1840*, London 1918.
10. Long, R.B., *Peninsular Cavalry General 1811–1813: The Correspondence of Lieutenant-General Robert Ballard Long*, ed. T.H. McGuffie, London 1951, p. 165.

thus mistook their nationality. (This was no idle fear; for example, in November 1811 Lieutenant Samuel King of the 13th Light Dragoons had been killed by a guerrilla who mistook him for a Frenchman.)

The delay between the promulgation of new regulations and the arrival of new uniforms in the field, as noted by Long, seems fairly typical. For example, the 16th Light Dragoons (serving in the Peninsula) received their new uniforms in December 1812. John Vandeleur of the 12th Light Dragoons recorded that their new uniforms had been received by December 1812, but their shakos took another month to arrive. He remarked that 'our neat little uniform is to be changed to that of a most foreign look.' A portrait by Thomas Heaphy of Frederick Ponsonby of the 12th, evidently based upon sketches executed in 1812, in fact shows an intermediate version of the uniform: the new jacket in combination with the old barrelled sash, breeches and Hessian boots, old-style pouch belt and black sword belt.[11] Some, in fact, never seem to have received the new uniform completely before the end of the Peninsular War. For example, Thomas Brotherton of the 14th Light Dragoons recalled that as late as 1814 he was still wearing the Tarleton helmet, 'that most cumbersome of all head-dresses, the bearskin helmet of the British Light Cavalry.'[12]

Despite some changes in head-dress and facing colours, the four hussar regiments (Plates 13, 15, 18 and 19) were not affected by the general reform of light cavalry uniform. The hussar uniform, however, did not meet with universal approbation because of its very decorative nature. Attempts to improve its practicality for campaign service, for example, brought forth this comment in the press in 1813:

> 'We are glad to find that the tiddy dol appearance of our hussar regiments has, at length, been noticed. That the ingenuity of our army milliners... should be exercised for the purpose of rendering the appearance of our brave fellows ridiculous instead of promoting their health and comfort and security, is much to be lamented... we cannot but think that the fribbling ornaments with which they are attired would better become an equestrian performer on one of our inferior stages, than a hardy veteran, when equipped for the field.'[13]

Nevertheless, almost two years later another newspaper described hussar uniform as 'a mere gee-gaw... subject, by its intrinsic frivolity, to public ridicule.'[14]

In particular, in their earlier Peninsular experiences, the fur hussar caps had not proved especially serviceable. Dr Adam Neale recorded that they were top-heavy, fell off during a charge and provided as much protection as cartridge paper, while Sir Robert Ker Porter wrote of the:

> 'muff-like appendages that encumber the heads of so many of our soldiers... this awkward cap of ours, by being constructed partly of pasteboard, soaks up a great quantity of wet... and so becomes unbearably heavy and disagreeable, while it affords no protection to the wearer. At all times they can be cut down to his skull with the greatest ease.'[15]

Consequently, the busbies were replaced by shakos for most regiments when the hussars returned to the Peninsula, as mentioned in the texts to Plates 13, 15 and 18.

The change in infantry uniform was neither so profound, nor so unpopular, as that affecting the cavalry. The principal alterations applied to head-dress and to officers' coats. In place of the officers' bicorn hats and the other ranks' 'stovepipe' shakos, a new shako was authorised for all ranks. Similarly, by General Order of 24 December 1811, the previous long-tailed coat worn by officers was replaced by

11. Collins, R.M., 'Colonel the Hon. Frederick Cavendish Ponsonby, 12th Light Dragoons', in *Journal of the Society for Army Historical Research*, Vol. XLVI (1968), pp. 1–5; also the source of the Vandeleur quotation.
12. Brotherton, T., *A Hawk at War: The Peninsular Reminiscences of General Sir Thomas Brotherton*, ed. B. Perrett, Chippenham 1986, p. 80.
13. *The Public Ledger*, 9 March 1813.
14. *The Statesman*, 7 January 1815.
15. Porter, Sir Robert Ker, *Letters from Portugal and Spain, Written During the March of the British Troops under Sir John Moore*, London 1809, p. 219; published under the nom-de-plume of 'An Officer'; reprinted Trotman, Cambridge 1985.

a short-tailed jacket based upon that worn by the other ranks, but double-breasted like the jackets worn already by officers of light infantry (the long-tailed coat and hat were retained for wear at court). Some were unsure of the new designs; for example, John Mills of the Coldstream Guards wrote that:

> 'We are all in consternation at the idea of the dress of the army being altered from cocked hats and coats to caps and jackets. Ye heavens, what will become of crooked legs, large heads, and still larger hinder parts?'[16]

The previously-quoted critic of the cavalry uniform, however, was much happier with the infantry proposals:

> 'I give every possible credit to all the alterations which have taken place. The cap is far better on service than the hat; and the jacket than the coat. The great coat, pantaloons, and gaiters, cannot be of a better colour, or more fit for service in the field; and the near resemblance to those of the men will undoubtedly be the means of saving many valuable lives.'[17]

The point that the new uniforms would make the officers less conspicuous, and therefore less likely to attract enemy fire, was indeed relevant. For example, at the attack on San Sebastian, Lieutenant Francis Maguire of the 4th Foot deliberately donned a bicorn with a prominent white plume, so that he would be easily visible to his own men (which Oman took as evidence that the other officers had adopted the new shakos by that time), but he made himself too conspicuous, and was killed.

The new shako, worn by all ranks, was the false-fronted type with the plume carried at the left side, as described in the text to Plate 26. Extant examples appear quite handsome, but it was not universally popular, and in some cases waterproof covers were worn at all times on campaign, which made it very undecorative. Notably, it did not show up well when compared with the smart and impressive head-dress worn by other Allied armies during the occupation of France after Waterloo. Writing of one occasion, Cavalié Mercer observed:

> 'Our infantry – indeed, our whole army – appeared at the review in the same clothes in which they had marched, slept, and fought for months. The colour had faded to a dusky brick-dust hue; their coats, originally not very smartly made, had acquired by constant wearing that loose easy set so characteristic of old clothes, comfortable to the wearer, but not calculated to add grace to his appearance. *Pour surcroit de laideur* [to increase the ugliness], their cap is perhaps the meanest, ugliest thing ever invented. From all these causes it arose that our infantry appeared to the utmost disadvantage – dirty, shabby, mean and very small.'[18]

Also in the regulations of 24 December 1811 was an order that officers were to wear, 'A grey cloth greatcoat corresponding in colour with that established for the Line, with a stand-up collar and a cape to protect the shoulders, and regimental buttons.' (See Plate 28) The 1802 regulations had specified a dark blue frock coat with red facings for officers, and in practice all manner of overcoats had been worn on campaign, making them conspicuous from the rank and file, as mentioned in one of the comments above. The December 1811 regulations also specified that, 'In the case of regiments on foreign service, the Officers are to wear grey pantaloons or overalls, with short boots, or with shoes and gaiters, such as the private men's.' A variety of overall-trousers had been worn on campaign, in a range of colours (grey, white or even blue). Blue, for example, was the colour worn by the 45th at Talavera, apparently uniquely at that battle. The universal pattern (shown, for example, in Plates 29, 30, 33 and 35) was

16. Mills, J., *For King and Country: The Letters and Diaries of John Mills, Coldstream Guards, 1811–14*, ed. I. Fletcher, Staplehurst 1995, p. 81.

17. *Royal Military Chronicle*, January 1813, p. 210.

18. Mercer, A.C., *Journal of the Waterloo Campaign*, Edinburgh & London 1870, Vol. II, p. 181; reprinted with Introduction by P. Haythornthwaite, Greenhill Books, London 1989, and by Da Capo Press, New York 1995.

evidently the result of a trial conducted during the Walcheren expedition, involving the 4th, 20th and 28th Foot.

'The 4th had them made tight, with black gaiters, the 20th, as overalls, with buttons down the sides, and the 28th loose, with half boots. On our return, they were compared; those of the 4th were all torn at the legs, the buttons were off the overalls of the 20th, while those of the 28th were nearly as good as when we started. The grey trousers, as first worn by the 28th regiment, were thus adopted throughout the army, to the great comfort of the soldier.'[19]

Implementation of the new uniform was in many cases probably considerably delayed; indeed, some units may have retained items of the previous uniform until almost the end of the Peninsular War. Units were re-uniformed periodically during the war, however (a practical necessity as clothing deteriorated to the point of raggedness under the exigencies of campaign), and the new uniforms sent to the army would conform to the latest regulations.

At this stage it is perhaps worth emphasising that the appearance of the army during a long campaign was often very much less impressive than that suggested by Hamilton Smith's plates, as uniforms became worn and stained.

Many contemporary accounts describe the deterioration of a unit's appearance, such as that recorded by William Wheeler of the 51st in January 1812:

'We were on duty every other night, our clothes worn thin and wrecked by the fatigues of the former Campaign. It was difficult to tell to what regiment we belonged, for each man's coat was like Joseph's "a coat of many colours".'[20]

Harry Ross-Lewin of the 32nd described his regiment in early 1814, when it was withdrawn temporarily from front-line service to receive new clothing:

'No one who had never before seen British troops could possibly have discovered at this period the original colour of our clothing; for it was so patched with a diversity of colours, and so bespoke a variety of wretchedness, that, with regard to this part of our equipment, we must have borne an undesirable resemblance to Falstaff's ragged regiment.'[21]

Frederick Mainwaring of the 51st probably spoke for many soldiers on campaign:

'No one thought about the cut of a coat, or the fashion of a boot, or looked coldly on his neighbour because his ragged garment was less fashionable than his own; sufficient was it that he had a coat on his back.'[22]

Officers' uniforms were purchased privately by each individual, but even in this case attempts seem to have been made to implement the new regulations. For example, as early as February 1812 tailors from England arrived in the Peninsula to measure the officers of the 28th for their new jackets, which at £5 16s (£5.80) each (exclusive of epaulette) would represent a considerable drain upon a subaltern's finances (it represented almost 18 days' pay for an infantry lieutenant, for example). Not every regiment was involved in the change, however. Officers of rifle corps were specifically excluded from the regulations of December 1811; light infantry officers already wore short jackets and shakos; and Highland regiments were also largely unaffected.

A system of officers' rank markings had been introduced by a General Order of 19 February 1810, by which field officers of infantry (including those of brevet rank but serving in a lesser role) were to

19. Cadell, C., *Narrative of the Campaigns of the 28th Regiment since their Return from Egypt in 1802*, London 1835, pp. 83–84.
20. Wheeler, W., *The Letters of Private Wheeler 1809–1828*, ed. B.H. Liddell Hart, London 1951, p. 74; reprinted Windrush 1994.
21. Ross-Lewin, H., *With the Thirty-Second in the Peninsula and other Campaigns*, ed. J. Wardell, Dublin & London 1904, p. 235.
22. Mainwaring, F., 'Four Years of a Soldier's Life', in *Colburn's United Service Magazine* 1844, Vol. II, p. 517.

wear two epaulettes with badges on the strap: a crown and a star for a colonel, a crown for a lieutenant-colonel, and a star for a major. Captains and subalterns had only one epaulette. For captains and above, the trimming was to be in bullion; for subalterns, fringe. The regulations of December 1811 confirmed these badges, extended their use to the new epaulettes of light dragoon officers, and added that field officers (including those of brevet rank) of fusiliers and light infantry would wear epaulettes on top of their flank company wings; and that the epaulettes of grenadiers would bear a grenade badge, and those of the light infantry a bugle-horn. However, the regulations of December 1811 also stated that, 'the epaulettes and wings of all regimental Officers are in future to be of the same description, without any other distinction' beyond the badges prescribed in February 1810. The meaning of this must have been unclear, for a Horse Guards letter of 14 April 1812 was necessary to elucidate the fact that, 'in conformity with the latest Regulations, Subaltern Officers were to wear bullion epaulettes', that is with bullion like captains and above, rather than the fringe prescribed in 1810, so that henceforth the epaulettes of captains and other subalterns would be indistinguishable. It is clear, however, that the wording of the December 1811 order was understood by some for, as early as February 1812, mention is made of subalterns ordering the new bullion-fringed epaulettes.

One of the most valuable parts of Hamilton Smith's work concerns not the 1812 changes specifically, but the designs of lace worn by the infantry rank and file. Information on the many different regimental patterns is not consistent; indeed, variations are recorded even in different copies of the Hamilton Smith charts (Plates 37–38), although they still remain a primary source for the designs of such lace.

The lace was applied to the collar, shoulder-straps, flank company wings, skirts, and as loops to each button, grouped either in pairs or set equidistantly (in threes for the Scots Guards). Usually the loops were square-ended (occasionally pointed as for the Coldstream Guards), or in an open 'bastion' shape (named after the traditional outline of such a fortification). Officially there were two varieties of 'bastion' loop, depending upon the width of the base, the wider 'Jew's harp' shape and the narrower 'flowerpot'; Hamilton Smith's charts do not seem to make any distinction between the two, although it is not certain if these shapes were entirely constant at the time. There were normally ten loops of lace upon the breast of the coat, though with the bastion design being wider, eight or nine was the usual number for these. All the lace was white, with a variety of interwoven coloured lines (entirely white for the Foot Guards). Some changes to lace design did occur during the period; for example, the 1st Foot changed from the square-ended loops in pairs shown in Plate 37 to single spaced bastion loops. (The coloured design of the 1st's lace is omitted from the copy of the chart which forms Plate 37: it was white with a blue 'double worm' which appeared like a chain-pattern. Details of other laces left uncoloured in this copy are given in the text to Plate 38.)

Because of the relatively small scale of the Hamilton Smith illustrations, details of the colouring of regimental lace are not always clear, so some elucidation is given below. Examples are also quoted of recorded variations to the designs shown on Plates 37–38, derived from several other sources including the 1802 draft of the clothing regulations, de Bosset's chart of 1803, the *Army List* and tailors' specifications, notably the records of the clothiers J.N. and B. Pearse,[23] although the details given in the last of these cannot be dated precisely.

From the Pearse records it appears that in Plates 37–38 the left-hand edge of the lace strip represents the 'inside' edge of a lace loop, and the right-hand side the 'outside' edge: for example, for the 4th Foot Pearse notes that the blue line was on the inside of the loop, and on the outside edge for the 7th Foot.

In the Hamilton Smith charts, it is not always easy to distinguish between blue and black stripes.

23. See Steppler, G.A., 'Redcoat: the Regimental Coat of the British Infantryman c. 1808–15', in *Military Illustrated* No. 22 (1989–90).

From other sources it appears that black stripes, rather than blue, were present in the lace of the 3rd, 9th, 12th, 20th, 28th, 32nd (plus black worm), 40th, 41st (or black worm), 43rd, 44th (with a blue and yellow stripe), 47th, 48th, 57th, 64th, 65th (with red and black worm), 68th, 70th, 76th, 80th, 85th, 88th and 91st. The red stripes of the 12th and 16th are specified elsewhere as being crimson, that for the 56th pink; the green stripe for the 63rd is described as being very small. The stripes for the 11th, 19th and 24th were red and green. Although confirmed elsewhere, Hamilton Smith's blue and yellow stripes for the 17th are described by Pearse as black and yellow (set at one edge, the plain edge outwards); and for the 65th, a black stripe near each edge.

For the 25th, Hamilton Smith shows the lace with the blue, red and yellow stripes which were worn when the facing colour was yellow, whereas Pearse indicates a blue 'wormed' stripe in the centre; perhaps the lace design was altered with or after the change to blue facings in 1805. Other recorded variations include: 31st, blue and yellow worm and small red stripes; 35th, yellow stripe; 34th, red stripe on inside, blue and yellow worn on outside; 38th, yellow stripe within two red; 46th, red and purple worm or red and blue stripe; 49th, one green and two red stripes; 52nd, red worm and orange stripe; 59th, red and yellow stripes; 66th, one green and one green and crimson stripe; 67th, yellow, purple and green stripes; 69th, red stripe between two green. The 1802 regulations indicate red and blue stripes for the 74th, Pearse one red stripe near the edge, and Hamilton Smith a red stripe on the inside of the loop. Pearse indicates that the 77th's lace had a red stripe near one edge, black and yellow stripes near the other, black outwards; 96th, red and yellow stripes along the inner edge, red outermost, and a black stripe on the outer edge; and the 97th, blue stripe between two yellow.

For sergeants the lace was plain white, the looping usually the same as for the other ranks, although sergeants of the Foot Guards had gold lace and it is thought that silver lace may have been worn by a few regiments. Instead of eight bastion loops on the breast, in pairs, like the rank and file, sergeants of the 22nd had ten square-ended loops, in pairs.

⸺⟫●⟪⸺

Studies concerning the uniforms and organisation of the regiments that wore them are not the place for remarks on the nature or characteristics of the soldiers who composed those armies; such information may be found in many of the works listed in the bibliography. Nevertheless, it is perhaps worth emphasising that the men whom Hamilton Smith portrayed so well were not mere cogs in the machinery of the line of battle.

Wellington's most familiar comment upon the ordinary soldiers who composed his army was made in the course of remarks concerning the French system of recruiting: 'The conscription calls out a share of every class no matter whether your son or my son – all must march; but our friends [the ordinary British soldiers] are the very scum of the earth.' Although a notable exaggeration, this remark seems not to have been made in any condemnatory manner, for on at least two occasions when he used the expression he added: 'It is only wonderful that we should be able to make so much out of them afterwards', and, 'you can hardly conceive such a set brought together, and it really is wonderful that we should have made them the fine fellows they are.'[24]

Reference to the myriad personal accounts of service in the British Army during the Napoleonic Wars will confirm the Duke's description of 'fine fellows', and that collectively they formed, as he was quoted earlier as remarking, 'probably the most complete machine for its numbers now existing in Europe'.

24. Stanhope, Earl, *Notes on Conversations with the Duke of Wellington 1831–1851*, London 1888, pp. 14, 18.

As a final comment – and one which concerns the uniforms and appearance of the army as portrayed by Hamilton Smith – it is interesting to note a story recorded by Cavalié Mercer in 1815. Following his description, quoted above, of the small stature of the British troops, exaggerated by their small shakos and their shabby, campaign-stained uniforms, when compared to the gorgeous dress worn by other Allied armies in Paris in 1815, he noted that their 'dirty, shabby and mean appearance' had, so it was said, been especially observed by the Allied sovereigns:

> 'A report has reached us this morning, that they remarked to the Duke what very small men the English were. "Ay", replied our noble chief, "they are small; but your Majesties will find none who fight so well".'[25]

---

25. Mercer, *Journal of the Waterloo Campaign*, Vol. II, pp. 181–82.

General Officers and Staff

Full Dress Uniform of a Field Marshal
(published 1 April 1812)

In its established form, the army's highest rank of field marshal dated from 1736, but after eleven appointments were made between that year and 1763 the rank was allowed to lapse. Following the death of the last, James O'Hara, 2nd Lord Tyrawley, in 1773, there were no field marshals until the appointment to that rank of three senior generals in October 1793. From then until the end of the French wars, fifteen more appointments were made, but they were largely honorific and at the conclusion of the Peninsular War only five field marshals were alive, four of whom were the sons of King George III. The senior was the king's second son, Frederick, Duke of York (1763–1827), who was the army's Commander-in-Chief 1795–1809 and 1811–27; he was appointed a field marshal on 10 February 1795. The others were Edward, Duke of Kent (1767–1820), appointed 5 September 1805, and Ernest, Duke of Cumberland (1771–1851) and Adolphus, Duke of Cambridge (1774–1850), both appointed on 26 November 1813. The fifth field marshal, something of an exception in that he held that rank while commanding troops in the field, was the Duke of Wellington, whose appointment was announced in the *London Gazette* of 3 July 1813 but backdated to 21 June, the day of the Battle of Vitoria, for which triumph the promotion was made.

The uniform of field marshals was not described officially until the *Dress Regulations* of 1831, so that portraits and illustrations like that shown here are of considerable value in determining exactly what they wore. For 'state' dress it appears that they had a single-breasted frock coat, replaced about 1814 by a coatee with much oak-leaf embroidery, though evidence is sparse. For ordinary full dress, as here, they wore a version of the standard general officers' uniform, a scarlet coatee with blue facings and gold-embroidered loops; Hamilton Smith shows ten or eleven loops on the breast, and six V-shaped loops on each sleeve (and presumably on the rear skirts), spaced evenly. It may be that this version of the coatee was introduced in 1811, when the previous two epaulettes were replaced by an aiguillette on the right shoulder, and this coat may have been replaced as early as 1814 by a version with slashed cuffs. The General Order of 24 December 1811 which regulated officers' uniforms described the hat shown: 'plain' (i.e. without gold lace edging) 'with the usual cord and tassels, with ostrich feathers around the brim. No other Officer or soldier of any description whatever, is to wear white feathers round the brim of the hat: this is henceforth to be considered the exclusive distinction of a General Officer.' The hat's cockade is held by what appears to be a version of the 'Star loop' which from 1811 was restricted otherwise to general officers of cavalry. Also shown here is a waist-belt with a plate bearing a reversed 'GR' cypher, supporting a sword with a boat-shaped shell guard and steel scabbard, similar to the type introduced for officers of heavy cavalry for full dress in 1796. At the date of publication of this plate, both the then existing field marshals (the Dukes of York and Kent) were holders of the Order of the Garter, the breast-star shown, although the plate is not stated to be a portrait. In the background may be seen members of the field marshal's staff, and a groom holding his charger with its gold-fringed, plain dark blue shabraque.

FULL-DRESS UNIFORM of A FIELD MARSHAL.

Drawn by C.H.S.

Aquatinted by I.C.Stadler

PLATE 2

Uniform of a Lieutenant General of Cavalry

(published 1 May 1813)

Holding the rank immediately below that of general, a lieutenant-general might command a division, or an army, on active service.

From about 1799, the earlier 'frock' coat worn by general officers had evolved into the coatee, on which the skirts were folded back to reveal part of the white lining as turnbacks. By 1802, when the 1768 Clothing Warrant was brought up to date, the principal ranks of general officer were distinguished by the design of embroidery they wore. For all ranks the scarlet coat was double-breasted, with dark blue facings (lapels, 'indented' cuffs – i.e. with a V-shaped upper edge – and front patch to the collar), and no pocket flaps. For full generals, there were nine gold-embroidered loops and gilt buttons upon each lapel, one upon each collar-patch, and four upon each cuff and skirt, spaced singly. For lower ranks, only the spacing of loops was specified, not the number: in threes for lieutenant-generals and in pairs for major-generals. For lieutenant-generals this usually meant nine loops on the breast, and six upon each sleeve and skirt, in groups of three, as shown in this plate. The lapels are shown in a popular style, folded back at the top, to expose some of the blue facing-colour; they might also be folded back to the waist, showing a plastron-like blue front, or fastened over completely at the top. Originally the coat was worn with epaulettes on both shoulders, consisting of scarlet straps bearing gold embroidery, and gold bullion fringes, but in 1811 these were replaced by a single aiguillette, in gold cord, upon the right shoulder. The regulations of 24 December 1811 note that general officers of cavalry were to wear the 'plain' hat with white ostrich-feather trim, as described in the text to Plate 1, with 'the Cavalry feather, with the Star loop' (hidden from view in this illustration). In addition to the staff uniform and cocked hat, as shown, the regulation noted that, 'When in command of Divisions or Brigades of Cavalry, they will be permitted to wear the Helmet of the Heavy Cavalry, with the Staff or Cavalry Uniform; a pouch-belt and a sabretache, which latter is to be fastened close to the sword-belt in the manner in which it is worn by the Heavy Cavalry.' As in Plate 1, the general depicted carries a sword resembling the full dress pattern of 1796 for officers of heavy cavalry.

In the background, the dragoon orderly holding the general's charger wears the revised version of the heavy cavalry helmet, with a horsehair mane falling from the comb which, as described in the Introduction (p. 31), replaced the original crested helmet shown in Plates 9 and 11.

UNIFORM OF A LIEUTENANT GENERAL OF CAVALRY.

PLATE 3

Major General of Infantry, Knight Commander of the Bath
(published April 1815)

An officer of the rank immediately below that of lieutenant-general, the major-general depicted wears the staff uniform described in the text to Plate 2, with rank indicated by the embroidered loops in pairs, including four loops upon each sleeve and skirt. The regulation of 24 December 1811 described the hat as resembling those mentioned previously, but that 'General Officers of Infantry are to wear the stand-up Infantry feather, with the scaled loop', the latter usually in gilt metal, but obscured in this view. Uniform distinctions for the lower rank of brigadier-general were first published in 1804, when it was specified that their coats should resemble those of major-generals, but for the loops on the sleeve and skirt, where instead of two pairs there should be three, set two over one, with the lowest sleeve-loop on the cuff. For all general officers the regulation button bore a crossed sword and baton surrounded by a laurel wreath in gilt; and in 1809 a further distinction was made in orders relating to the appointment of colonel of the staff, whose coat was to resemble that of a brigadier but with the staff button which bore an abstract, hatched design. The order of 1811 which replaced epaulettes with the single aiguillette must have applied to brigadiers, but colonels on the staff are not mentioned, and as the regulations of 1822 state that they wore two epaulettes, presumably they never used the aiguillette but wore epaulettes throughout.

In addition to the embroidered coats shown in Plates 1–3, all general and staff officers could wear a 'plain' coat, in which the gold-embroidered loops were replaced by stitched lines of coloured thread, sometimes described as 'twist loops', matching the colour of the cloth upon which they were set, and in the same arrangement as the gold loops. An example of the plain coat is worn by the mounted figure in the background of this plate, whose single gold epaulette on the right shoulder identifies him as an aide-de-camp to a general of infantry (see the text to Plate 5).

The Order of the Bath was the principal military decoration for officers, founded by King George I in 1725 in its present form, with its membership enlarged greatly on 2 January 1815 to reward deserving officers from the late war. Its first class, Knights Grand Cross, was limited to 60 military and 12 civilian members; its second class, Knights Commanders, was not to exceed 180 men (plus ten honorary appointments of foreign officers holding British commissions); and members of its third class were Commanders of the order. A Knight Commander wore the cross of the order upon a red ribbon around the neck, and an embroidered star upon the left breast, as shown here; of the first 160 appointed in 1815, 37 held the rank of major-general (plus four honorary members from the King's German Legion), of whom the senior was Major-General Alan Cameron of Erracht, a general officer from July 1810 and colonel of the 79th Regiment, which he had raised.

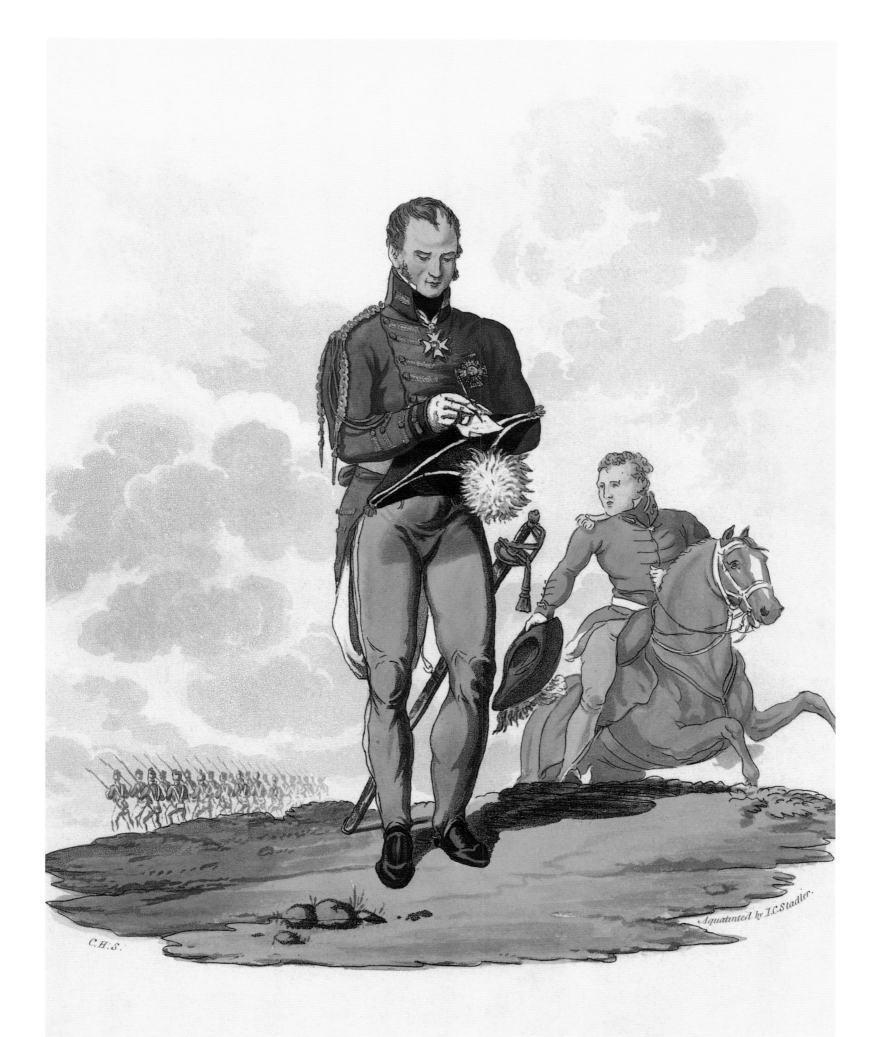

MAJOR GENERAL of INFANTRY.

KNIGHT COMMANDER of the BATH.

Staff of the Army: Quarter Master General, or Adjutant General (not being General Officers); Ass[istan]t Quarter Master General or Ass[istan]t Adjutant General; Soldiers of the Royal Staff Corps [R to L]

(published January 1813)

This plate depicts various members of the administrative departments of the army, which played a vital role on campaign; as described in the Introduction (pp. 13–14), most regular staff duties were divided between the departments of the Adjutant-General and the Quartermaster-General.

The uniform of adjutant- and quartermaster-generals was specified by an order of 1799, which directed them to wear the same uniform as a lieutenant-general, and a deputy adjutant- or quartermaster-general that of a major-general, but with silver embroidery instead of gold; with a silver epaulette on the left shoulder only, unless on the king's staff, when two epaulettes were worn. Those of the rank of general officer were permitted to use the general officers' design of button, in silver, and those below that rank the staff button, in silver. The mounted figure here is a QMG or AG on the king's staff, and although the embroidery upon the lapels is not shown clearly to be in groups of three, the loops on the skirt and sleeve are, matching the rank-marking of lieutenant-general.

The uniform of assistant adjutant- and quartermaster-generals was described by a General Order of May 1804, which specified a single-breasted coat with blue collar and cuffs, and embroidered silver loops: eleven on the breast, one upon the collar and four upon each skirt and sleeve, spaced evenly; with two silver lace epaulettes upon scarlet straps. This is the uniform worn by the dismounted officer in this plate, although his collar is scarlet with a blue patch, which may indicate an officer on the king's staff.

The two 'other ranks' in the background belong to the Royal Staff Corps, a unit established in 1798 to provide a force of engineers under the control of the army (the ordinary engineering services being controlled by the Master-General of the Ordnance). The initial four companies were expanded to battalion strength in 1809; its members were all trained as infantrymen in addition to their constructional skills, and were intended to be employed as overseers or foremen for gangs of labourers drawn from the infantry. The privates were divided into three classes, the 1st class to act as sergeants, the 2nd as corporals and 3rd as lance-corporals. The officers were often employed on detached duty in a wide range of engineering or staff roles. The uniform was similar to that of the infantry, in red with blue facings, with white piping to the facings instead of lace loops, and no tufts on the shoulder straps. As visible here, a badge of '1' or '2' was borne upon the left upper arm, indicating 1st or 2nd class private. They wore blue pantaloons with short gaiters, and clothing instructions for 1812 mention grey pantaloons, half boots, a 'round jacket' and grey trousers, probably for working dress. The men illustrated wear a shoulder belt for the cartridge box and a waist belt for the bayonet, instead of the two shoulder belts of the infantry, and sergeants were noted as carrying swords and shoulder belts, and wearing sashes, like infantry sergeants.

STAFF OF THE ARMY,

QUARTER MASTER GENENERAL, or ADJUTANT GENERAL,

(not being General Officers)

ASS.^T QUARTER MASTER GENERAL or ASS.^T ADJUTANT GENERAL

SOLDIERS of the ROYAL STAFF CORPS.

Aquatinted by I.C. Stadler

PLATE 5

An Aid[e] de Camp [L], and Brigade Major of Cavalry [R]

(published September 1812)

Illustrated here are two of the more junior appointments of staff officer. Aides-de-camp were young officers appointed to the staff of a general (often termed his 'family', a small and close group) to assist him and to act as couriers to carry his messages. Somewhat unfairly, it was said that such duty required only courage and horsemanship: for example, in 1810 Harry Smith joked that although he had an injured ankle, he was perfectly fit to serve as an ADC because 'I can ride and eat!'[1] The latter comment refers to the fact that, although each general was allowed one ADC at government expense, lieutenant-generals two and a force commander three, subsistence for additional ADCs had to be financed from the general's own pocket. Not infrequently ADCs were a general's relatives or the sons of his friends; in the Waterloo campaign, for example, Lord Hill's senior ADC was his brother, Sir Henry Clinton's was his nephew, and three of the four ADCs to the Earl of Uxbridge were officers of his own regiment.

The uniform of ADCs was prescribed in 1799 as resembling that of assistants in the Adjutant-General's and Quartermaster-General's departments, but decorated in gold: a scarlet coat with dark blue facings, single-breasted, with embroidered loops on the breast, one on the collar and three on each sleeve and skirt, with an epaulette on the right shoulder for ADCs to infantry generals, on the left for cavalry, and two epaulettes for an ADC to the Commander-in-Chief. By the order of 24 December 1811 ADCs to cavalry generals were ordered to replace their epaulette with an aiguillette on the right shoulder (as shown here). In December 1814 new regulations specified that an ADC to the Commander-in-Chief would wear two epaulettes and an aiguillette on the right, with extra embroidery around the collar and down the front opening of the coat; for an ADC to a commander of a force abroad, two epaulettes; and for an ADC to a general of cavalry and infantry, a single epaulette on the left and right shoulder respectively. (Even if they were of field rank themselves, with the above exceptions ADCs could wear only a single epaulette.) Their buttons were plain gilt.

The duties of a major of brigade (or brigade-major) were explained as being equivalent to the tasks of an adjutant-general within the formation to which he was attached: he transmitted the orders of the adjutant-general to the units in his own brigade, and conveyed a daily report of these units to the adjutant-general's department, and, 'As all orders pass through the hands of the majors of brigade they have many opportunities of displaying their talents and proving their exactness.'[2] Their uniform was first prescribed, in 1799, as like that of ADCs but with silver embroidery and plain silver buttons. The regulations concerning the use of epaulettes applied equally to brigade majors, those appointed to the cavalry wearing a silver aiguillette on the right shoulder between the orders of December 1811 and those of December 1814 which reintroduced the epaulette on the left shoulder instead of the aiguillette.

1. *The Autobiography of Sir Harry Smith 1787–1819*, ed. G.C. Moore Smith, London 1910, p. 35; reprinted with Introduction by P.J. Haythornthwaite, Constable, London 1999.
2. *The British Military Library or Journal*, London 1801, Vol. II, p. 477.

Aquatinted by I C Stadler

CHS

AN AID DE CAMP, AND BRIGADE MAJOR OF CAVALRY.

The Cavalry

PLATE 6
An Officer of the 2[n]d Regiment of Life Guards in Full Dress
(published July 1812)

Tracing their origin to troops of horse which had followed King Charles II into exile, the Life Guards were the most senior corps in the British Army, reorganised into two regiments in 1788. The uniform shown here is the old full dress, which probably remained in use for royal escorts and state occasions for some time after the adoption, in 1812, of a more practical uniform suited for active service. The regimental facing colour was dark blue, though here the lapels are covered by gold lace, the cuffs concealed by the gauntlets, and the collar is shown as scarlet, which was apparently a distinction of the 2nd Life Guards, the 1st wearing blue. (Hamilton Smith's chart, Plate 23, shows a blue collar for the 1st Regt. and red with a blue patch for the 2nd, neither detail conforming with Plates 6 and 7.) The gold lace chevrons on sleeves and skirts were an old decoration used by the heavy cavalry. In both Plates 6 and 7, dress horse furniture is shown (the crowned Garter star badge illustrated here being an old insignia of the regiment); for active service a sheepskin saddle cover was used, black for officers and white for other ranks, with red or blue edging for the 1st and 2nd Life Guards respectively. The sword illustrated here has a broad, hatchet-pointed blade like that carried by the other ranks (the 1796 heavy cavalry pattern), but for officers the hilt was more complex, in steel, of semi-basket style, with slots cut into the guard which had given rise to its description as 'ladder-hilted'. The officers' dress pattern of 1796 was like that shown in Plates 1–3.

As mentioned in the Introduction (p. 15), in 1812 it was decided to send service squadrons of the Household Cavalry to the Peninsula, whereupon a new uniform was devised, probably quite similar to that shown in Plate 7, including a short-tailed jacket, blue and yellow girdle (crimson and gold for officers), grey overalls and a helmet. The helmet was authorised on 12 March 1812 and was similar to the pattern finally adopted by heavy cavalry in 1812, and worn by the dragoon orderly in Plate 2. Constructed of black leather, it had a brass comb, a border of brass scales, and a brass front-plate bearing a crowned, reversed 'GR' cypher over an oval plaque inscribed with the regimental title, brass chin-scales and a flowing, black horsehair mane falling from the comb. The metalwork was gilt for officers. In 1814 this uniform was amended to that shown in Plates 7 and 8.

In May 1814 it was ordered that the long coats be retained for the royal 'Drawing Rooms', but that officers should wear the new jackets, in conjunction with white breeches and jack boots, even at the Prince Regent's Levée. Also in 1814, an experiment was made when members of the 2nd Life Guards were issued with black-enamelled cuirasses (with gilded decorations for officers) for ceremonial duty, but they did not find favour and were discontinued almost immediately.

AN OFFICER *of the* 2.ᵈ REGIMENT *of* LIFE GUARDS.
in full Dress.

PLATE 7

First Regiment of Life Guards, New Uniform

(published May 1815)

As mentioned in the text to Plate 6, a new uniform was introduced when the Life Guards sent their service squadrons to the Peninsula, where they served from early 1813; and another new uniform was introduced in 1814 and worn during the Waterloo campaign.

Instead of the helmet with horsehair mane, a similar pattern was introduced, but with a worsted crest of crimson sandwiched between dark blue or black, with a white-over-red plume at the left. The brass fittings were similar to those on the maned helmet, including comb, scales at the sides and front plate, as described in the text to Plate 6, but apparently the helmets of the Life Guards had brass peaks. Officers' helmets had gilt fittings and a silk crest. Two short-tailed, scarlet jackets were designed, of which the dress or 'laced' version is shown here. It had blue gauntlet cuffs and turnbacks, and probably usually a scarlet collar with blue patch, as shown, although all-blue collars are recorded (and indicated for the 1st Regiment in the chart, Plate 23). The breast fastened with hooks and eyes and was ornamented with vertical strips of lace, gold for officers and probably an inferior type of gold for other ranks. Similar lace edged the cuffs and turnbacks, and other ranks' shoulder straps were formed from it; officers had narrow, twisted gold braid straps. The undress or 'frock' uniform, as worn during the Waterloo campaign, was similar, but with blue round cuffs, the collar patch and cuff with two gold loops each, and ten buttons instead of lace down the breast. Other ranks had blue shoulder straps, and officers the twisted braid straps, although a portrait of a 2nd Life Guards officer shows gold epaulettes.

White breeches and long boots were worn for state occasions or for attendance on the royal family, otherwise grey overalls with a gold (dress) or scarlet (undress) stripe; other ranks wore plain grey or grey with a red stripe. The girdle was yellow with two scarlet stripes; for officers, gold with three crimson stripes. Belts were white leather, covered with gold lace for officers for dress, their rectangular gilt plates bearing a silver Garter star. For officers their dress pouch and sabretache were faced with blue velvet, edged with gold lace and bore an embroidered Garter star, backed by a trophy of arms and surmounted by a crown; for undress, pouch and sabretache were black leather, bearing a small, gilt royal crest. Other ranks' sabretaches bore a brass, eight-pointed star with a reversed 'GR' cypher in the centre, and their pouches a large, oval brass plate bearing the royal coat of arms. The sword illustrated is the 1796 pattern heavy cavalry sabre with a straight, hatchet-tipped blade; prior to the Waterloo campaign it was ordered that the tips be ground to a point, probably with the intention of piercing the breastplates of the French cuirassiers, who had never before been engaged by British troops. As noted in the text to Plate 6, the dress horse furniture is shown here. In the background of this plate is a trumpeter in gold-laced state dress, very similar to the state uniform still worn by Household Cavalry trumpeters and bandsmen.

FIRST REGIMENT of LIFE GUARDS.

NEW UNIFORM.

C.H.S.

Aquatinted by I.C.Stadler.

Plate 8
Royal Horse Guards, Blues
(published November 1814)

Generally regarded as part of the Household Cavalry, the regiment traced its origin to the Royal Regiment of Horse, formed in January 1661, though its antecedents were even more ancient. Its first colonel was Aubrey de Vere, 20th Earl of Oxford, who was dismissed briefly by King James II but re-appointed by William III after the Glorious Revolution. From their colonel, and the colour of their uniform, they took the sobriquet 'Oxford Blues', initially to distinguish them from William III's 'Dutch Blue Guards', but as they retained the blue coat, and were the only regiment of cavalry so dressed, the appellation 'Blues' continued to be used (and is part of the official title of their modern descendants, The Blues and Royals).

Originally the regiment wore the long-tailed cavalry uniform with cocked hat (similar to those in Plate 6, but the coat blue with red facings and gold lace), but a more practical uniform was designed when it was decided to send a detachment to the Peninsula in 1812. This probably resembled that of the Life Guards, but it is known that they had not received the new helmets before their departure. (Nevertheless, the appearance of the Household Cavalry in Spain was described as being 'as fair and beautiful as lilies',[1] when contrasted with the battered appearance of those who had been many years on campaign, who made jokes about the Householders' fresh and well-fed look).

Apparently the Blues never received the maned helmet, but wore the caterpillar-crested version from the time their bicorns were replaced; consequently, when the Life Guards replaced the maned version, the Blues' worsted-crested helmet was quoted as their future pattern. For other ranks the peak was black leather with brass binding, but metal for officers (although the portrait of Captain William R. Clayton, c. 1815, shows a leather peak). For 'dress', the Blues wore a short-tailed jacket like that of the Life Guards, in blue with scarlet facings and gold lace; for both officers and other ranks, the collar was edged with lace and bore a single loop, and as shown here, the other ranks' lace had a central red stripe. Hamilton Smith shows scarlet epaulettes with gold fringe; these were not worn by officers, and conceivably those shown here may have been a mark of NCO rank. It is known (from the extant uniform worn at Waterloo by Sir Robert Hill) that officers had an undress jacket with buttons down the front, as worn by the Life Guards but in the Blues' colouring, with lace loops only upon the collar and cuffs, and although there is no direct evidence, presumably the rank and file wore something similar during the Waterloo campaign.

In most other respects their uniform and equipment resembled those of the Life Guards, although buff-coloured breeches and belts were traditional for the regiment – note here the crimson 'flask cord' carried along the pouch belt – and as just visible here, the Blues used S-shaped belt clasps instead of the rectangular plates used by other heavy cavalry. Their service dress overalls had red stripes (double stripes for officers, whose dress pantaloons had two gold stripes, piped scarlet), and although the sabretaches of the rank and file had no badges, those of the officers resembled the dress pattern of the Life Guards, but with scarlet backing to the decorations.

1. Leach, J, *Rough Sketches of the Life of an Old Soldier*, London 1831, p. 300; reprinted Trotman, London 1986.

ROYAL HORSE GUARDS,

Blues.

PLATE 9
A Private of the 1st or King's Dragoon Guards
(published March 1812)

The senior regiment of line cavalry was created in 1685 as the Queen's Regiment of Horse; it received the title of 1st (King's) Dragoon Guards in 1746. It served in Flanders 1793–95, but its only subsequent service during the Napoleonic Wars was at Waterloo, brigaded with the Household Cavalry.

The new regulations introduced quite radical changes in the uniform of the cavalry. For the heavy regiments (dragoon guards and dragoons) the previous long-tailed coat was replaced by a short-tailed, single-breasted red jacket, sometimes referred to by the German term *collet*. The regimental facing-colour was carried upon the collar, cuffs and turnbacks; the cuffs were of 'gauntlet' pattern for dragoon guards (here covered by gloves) and pointed for dragoons, and for officers of dragoon guards the facings were velvet. The garment was closed by hooks and eyes, and down the breast was vertical yellow or white lace (according to the colour of the buttons) with a coloured stripe in the centre; similar lace edged the cuffs and turnbacks and formed the shoulder straps (officers' lace was gold or silver respectively, with twisted cord shoulder-decoration). For dragoons, the breast-lace continued up the front of the collar; dragoon guards had red collar patches instead, as shown here and in Plate 23.

The white breeches and high boots shown continued to be worn for 'dress' occasions until they were discontinued, by an order of September 1815, in favour of ankle-boots and dark grey or blue-grey overalls similar to the service dress overalls worn previously; for other ranks these are usually shown as having two red stripes, and for officers one or two gold or silver stripes (according to the regimental lace-colour). The rank and file wore a yellow girdle with two stripes of the facing colour (for regiments with a pale facing-colour, red stripes seem to have been used). Officers wore a gold girdle or sash with three crimson stripes, or a plain crimson sash for undress. The officers' regulations of 24 December 1811 specified that they should wear laced jackets like those of the other ranks, and:

> 'a small sabretache fastened close to the sword-belt in a manner similar to the men's, with the sash at present worn by the Heavy Cavalry, tied on the left side. When at a Drawing Room or Levée, they are to wear long coats as at present, with an aiguillette on the right shoulder, and a cocked hat with a Star loop.'[1]

Shown here is the first pattern of helmet; it is described in the text to Plate 11, and its replacement is noted in the Introduction (p. 31). Also shown here is the full dress horse furniture, with 'housings' of the facing colour, edged with regimental lace. Although not shown very clearly, the regimental insignia in the corners consisted of a crowned, reversed 'GR' cypher, over 'KD' over 'G', the same lettering appearing on the end of the tubular scarlet valise carried at the rear of the saddle. The carbine is shown with its lock covered and its muzzle in the 'boot' attached to the horse furniture, the stock supported by a strap around the pommel of the saddle. It could also be suspended from the shoulder belt, from the spring-clip shown.

---

1. See Sumner, Revd. P., 'Officers' Dress Regulations, 1811', in *Journal of the Society for Army Historical Research* Vol XXII (1944), pp. 339–40.

Etched by C.H.S

Aquatinted by I.C.Stadler.

A PRIVATE of the 1ST or KINGS DRAGOON GUARDS.

PLATE 10

A Private of the 2d or Royal North British Dragoons (Greys)

(published December 1813)

The only cavalry regiment with a distinctly Scottish identity (and the most distinctive head-dress), the 2nd Dragoons originated with independent companies of dragoons raised in Scotland in 1678 and formed into a regiment by Lieutenant-General Thomas Dalyell of the Binns in 1681. Although known as 'Scots Greys', that name was not taken into the regiment's official title until 1866, but probably was derived from the colour of their horses, which were first mentioned as being exclusively greys in 1693–94. After service in Flanders in 1793–95, the regiment did not go on campaign again until 1815, where it won great fame as part of the 'Union' Brigade at Waterloo; it was during its charges that Sergeant Charles Ewart captured the Eagle of the French 45th Line, one of the most celebrated incidents from the battle.

In common with the other dragoon regiments, the Greys adopted the uniform described in the text to Plate 9; the pointed cuffs are shown clearly here. Although the chart (Plate 23) shows the other ranks' lace as white, it was ordered to be changed to yellow in October 1811 to match the gold lace of the officers, and it is the yellow lace which is shown correctly here. The figure in the background wears the grey overalls used on service; other sources show a double rather than single blue stripe.

The distinction of wearing grenadier caps was presumably an extension of their use by a regimental grenadier company; they are mentioned as early as October 1705 which seems to disprove the old story that they were adopted after the regiment defeated French grenadiers at Ramillies (23 May 1706). Grenadier caps were noted as being worn by the whole regiment in the 1751 Clothing Warrant, made of cloth until fur caps were introduced by the Warrant of 1768, although it was not until June 1778 that they were actually adopted by the Greys. By the early 19th century the fur cap had evolved into the type shown here, with a peak, brass front plate, a white plume at the left side, and upon the rear of the cap a white horse of Hanover upon a red cloth patch. Like other cavalry head-dress, it could be worn with a blackened, waterproof cover. After Waterloo a brass scroll bearing that battle honour was added above the front plate.

Heavy cavalry equipment included a wide, whitened leather belt over the shoulder, supporting both the cartridge pouch and carbine upon its spring-clip. The waist belt bore a rectangular brass plate emblazoned with the regimental insignia, with four slings, two each for the sabre and sabretache, the latter in plain black leather like the pouch. Officers had lace-covered belts, and embroidered versions of the sabretache for full dress, generally of the facing colour, edged with regimental lace and bearing embroidered regimental symbols. Their sabretaches were carried on three slings. For undress they had white leather belts and black leather sabretaches, and for both belts used a rectangular gilt plate bearing a crowned royal cypher within a laurel wreath, upon a scroll inscribed 'Dieu et Mon Droit', all in silver.

A PRIVATE OF THE 2ᴰ OR ROYAL NORTH BRITISH DRAGOONS *(GREYS.)*

C.H.S.

Aquatinted by I.C.Stadler.

Plate 11

A Private of the 3rd or King's Own Dragoons
(published April 1812)

Created by the regimentation of some independent companies in 1685, this regiment was granted the title 'King's Own' and was numbered as the 3rd Regiment of Dragoons in 1751. It remained as the 3rd (King's Own) Dragoons until 1818, when it was converted to light dragoons. It saw considerable service during the Napoleonic Wars, at Walcheren in 1809 and in the Peninsula from 1811 until the end of the war, for which service it was awarded the battle honours for Salamanca, Vitoria and Toulouse in addition to the universal honour 'Peninsula'.

This plate shows more details of the heavy cavalry uniform described in the text to Plates 9 and 10. Shown clearly here are the pointed cuffs of the dragoons, and the regimental devices upon the 'dress' horse furniture, a crowned Garter over 'KO' over 'D'. It was ordered in 1811 that the heavy cavalry should buckle their sabretaches high, though some illustrations show them hanging about calf-level, in the fashion adopted by the light regiments.

The most notable feature of this plate – and of Plate 9 – is the helmet, which is the pattern ordered initially to replace the previous cocked hat. The new head-dress was made of black felt with a brass peak and brass reinforcing bars on the sides, a brass front-plate and a brass comb supporting a worsted 'caterpillar' crest. The warrant for its introduction was dated 12 March 1812, and its approval was dated 20 March, but as Hamilton Smith's plates which depict it are dated March (Plate 9) and April 1812 (Plate 11), obviously he must have been copying one of the experimental manufactures, for an issue of helmets could not have been made so rapidly after the date of official approval. This may explain variations in the depictions of the crest: Plate 9 shows a crest of black over red, while Hamilton Smith's 3rd Dragoon has a black crest; a picture of the same regiment by Denis Dighton[1] has a blue crest with transverse red stripes. Sample head-dress presented to the Prince of Wales described the helmets as having a felt skull (beaver for officers), brass scales around the base, front plates bearing a 'double GR and crown', and crests of black and red worsted (silk for officers).[2] Some helmets of this pattern *were* issued, for in October 1812 the commanding officer of the 6th Dragoon Guards was informed by the War Office that his men should not be compelled to pay for the feather plumes to the new helmets, which had proved 'in every way objectionable', and were to be replaced by a revised pattern of helmet governed by the regulation then in force, the Warrant of 12 March having been cancelled.[3] The new pattern, with a horsehair mane as described in the Introduction (p. 31), was apparently approved in August 1812, but it may be that its first issue may have been made a short while earlier. Hamilton Smith subsequently produced revised 'states' of both Plates 9 and 11, showing the maned helmet, and it is also depicted in Plate 2.

1. See Haswell Miller, A.E., and Dawnay, N.P., *Military Drawings and Paintings in the Royal Collection*, Vol. I, London 1966, fig. 300.
2. See Norman, A.V.B., 'Regulation Head-Dresses of the British Army, 1812', in *Journal of the Society for Army Historical Research*, Vol. XLIX (1971), pp. 38–9.
3 For the full text of the order see Sumner, Revd. P., 'A Special Copy of Hamilton Smith', in *ibid.*, Vol. XXVIII (1950), p. 14.

A PRIVATE *of the* 3.ᴿᴰ *or* KINGS OWN DRAGOONS.

Etched by C.H.S.

Plate 12
Uniform of a Major General of Light Dragoons
(published August 1813)

This plate is a rare depiction of one of the most unusual uniforms in the collection, combining elements of staff uniform with the new dress of light dragoons. The officers' dress regulations of 24 December 1811 noted that general officers of light dragoons were:

> 'When in the field, to wear blue jackets faced with scarlet, and embroidered with gold, according to their respective ranks, and made according to the pattern established for Light Dragoons; a crimson and gold sash, same as the Officers of Light Dragoons, sabretache, pouch and chakos. When attending a Drawing Room or Levée, they may appear in the Staff Uniform of their rank, with cocked hat, or in the Dress above described.'

This is the uniform shown here, based upon that of officers of light dragoons (see Plates 14 and 17), with embroidered 'staff' loops on the breast, evidently in pairs, indicating the rank of major-general. The hanging 'bag' on the shako, however, is a singular decoration. A further item of 'staff' insignia is the crossed sabre and scabbard on the sabretache, beneath the crowned and reversed 'GR' cypher. The sword carried by the major-general is of a similar pattern, the 'Mameluke' style which, as suggested by its name, originated largely with the campaign in Egypt in 1801, following which the weapons of the Mameluke warriors were adopted and later copied by European sword-cutlers. The style was very fashionable despite the lack of protection afforded to the hand by the simple quillons and absence of a knucklebow, but at this date it was unregulated; the first regulation sword of this oriental model was the 1822 pattern for lancer officers, and not until 1831 was the Mameluke sabre prescribed officially for general officers.

Rather more common than this are depictions of the special uniform of general officers of hussars, and examples of their costume are still extant. Although following the usual hussar style, the generals' uniform was unique in having a scarlet dolman and breeches, dark blue pelisse, a profusion of gold lace and either a tall fur cap or, more rarely, a shako. (The December 1811 regulations merely note that with the established uniform, at a drawing room or levée, generals of hussars were to wear 'scarlet pantaloons ornamented with gold'.) The uniform is shown in several portraits including those of the Prince Regent, the Marquess of Anglesey, the Marquess of Londonderry (better-known in the Napoleonic Wars as General Charles William Stewart), Sir Hussey Vivian, Lord Combermere and the Duke of Cumberland, and it was even worn with the Allied Army of the North in 1813. Some of these illustrations depict yellow boots, one of the most decorative items worn by hussar officers in full dress.

UNIFORM of a MAJOR GENERAL of LIGHT DRAGOONS.

Plate 13

A Private of the 7th or Queen's Own L[ight] D[ragoons] (Hussars)
(published August 1813)

The 7th Light Dragoons originated in 1690, with the formation into a regiment of previously independent troops of horse. Titled as the Queen's Own Dragoons from 1727 and numbered as the 7th from 1751, it was converted to light dragoons in 1784 and to hussars in 1806, although the regimental title was still officially 'Light Dragoons', with the term 'Hussars' added in parentheses. (Regiments of light cavalry dressed in hussar uniform were fashionable in many European armies, in an attempt to replicate the skill and élan of the Hungarian light horse who were the original hussars.) The regiment served in Flanders in 1793–95, in North Holland in 1799, and in the Corunna campaign (1808–09). It returned to the Peninsula in September 1813 and served with the hussar brigade, and fought at Waterloo. From 1801 it had the great distinction of having as its colonel Henry William Paget, Earl of Uxbridge and later Marquess of Anglesey (1768–1854), one of the best cavalry commanders of his generation.

The conversion from light dragoons to hussars did not involve too radical a change of uniform, for the tail-less blue jacket, with horizontal lines of braid upon the breast, continued to be worn by the four regiments which were transformed into hussars, and unlike the ordinary light dragoons these jackets were retained even after the uniform changes of 1811–12. (Comments on the hussar uniform in general are included in the Introduction p. 33.) To this they added the characteristic hussar appendages of a tall fur cap (busby), the braided, fur-edged over-jacket (pelisse), 'barrelled' sash and sabretache (although the latter had been adopted already by some light dragoons). Distinctive features worn by the 7th included the white fur on the pelisse (brown for officers) and the blue and white sash. Hamilton Smith shows both facing colour and braid as white, both here and in Plate 23, although by the date of publication of Plate 13 both had been changed: in 1811 it was ordered that the regiment should change from white to yellow lace, and their facings to blue in the following year. New uniforms incorporating these changes seem to have been issued between the second half of 1812 and the beginning of 1813, but the old uniform with white lace seems to have been worn when the regiment returned to the Peninsula in the autumn of 1813.

As mentioned in the Introduction (p. 33), the regiment was among those hussar units which adopted shakos in place of the busby; for the 7th the shakos were covered in blue cloth (with yellow lace for privates, gold for sergeants and presumably officers, according to contemporary records, but red shakos for the regimental band). Hamilton Smith shows the service overalls as grey, with a double white stripe; subsequently these were replaced by blue, with a single yellow stripe. It was these which were worn in the Waterloo campaign, together with the new, blue-faced jacket with yellow braid, and with the busby, the shakos by that date having worn out.

C.H.S.

Aquatinted by I.C.Stadler.

A PRIVATE *of the* 7TH *or* QUEENS OWN L.D.(HUSSARS.)

PLATE 14

An Officer of the IXth Light Dragoons in Review Order
(published March 1812)

Raised in 1715, the 9th Regiment of Dragoons was converted to Light Dragoons in 1783. The regiment spent almost the whole of the 18th century in Ireland, serving there during the 1798 rebellion (including at the action at Vinegar Hill). It took part in the disastrous foray to South America and in the expedition to Walcheren, and went to the Peninsula in the summer of 1811, serving at Arroyo dos Molinos. It was sent home in March/April 1813, with its horses being distributed among the regiments that remained, and did not serve in the Waterloo campaign. In 1816 the 9th was converted to lancers and not until 1830 was it accorded a royal title, as the 9th (or Queen's Royal) Light Dragoons (Lancers).

This plate illustrates the uniform designed for light dragoons in 1811 and issued from the beginning of 1812: the 9th wore the previous uniform when it went to the Peninsula, but as early as February 1812 some newly-arrived officers had the new uniform, and the regiment in general was re-clothed in November 1812. In place of the previous braided jacket and 'Tarleton' helmet (as shown in Plates 40–42) the new uniform consisted of a short-tailed jacket with the facing colour borne upon the collar, pointed cuffs, lapels and turnbacks, with piping of the same colour on the rear seams. When fastened back, as here, the lapels were closed with hooks and eyes; for marching order they were buttoned across, so that only the blue side was visible. There were ten buttons on each lapel, two at the rear of each cuff, and three on each vertical pocket flap on the skirts. Officers wore two epaulettes, with badges of rank upon the strap, and a strip of bullion fringe or 'waterfall' at the rear waist, in the regimental button colour; the epaulettes were white, or yellow for other ranks.

The new head-dress was a shako, wider at the top than the base, with a lace upper band and a cockade, connected by a vertical loop to a lace circlet on the front, for officers resembling a wheel with 'spokes' of thin braid, with the national white over red plume. The lace was in the button colour, but for all regiments the cap-lines were yellow (gold and crimson for officers). Further details of the new uniform are given in the text to Plate 17. For the 9th, regimental distinctions had included buff facings and silver lace, but in 1811 these were changed to the crimson facings and gold lace shown here.

Also illustrated here is the officers' horse furniture: a black sheepskin with red edging, and for dress occasions a dark blue shabraque edged with the regimental lace and bearing in the corners a crowned, reversed 'GR' cypher over the regimental initials (here 'IX.L' over 'D'), with a tubular valise decorated in the same manner.

AN OFFICER of the IXTH LIGHT DRAGOONS.

IN REVIEW ORDER.

PLATE 15

A Corporal of the 10th or Prince of Wales's Own Royal Hussars in Review Order

(published January 1813)

One of the most prestigious regiments in the army, by virtue of its royal connections, the 10th had received the title 'Prince of Wales's Own' in 1783, and such was the Prince's interest in 'his' regiment that he was appointed to the post of 'colonel commandant' in 1793, and on 18 July 1796 became its colonel when the previous incumbent, General Sir William Augustus Pitt, transferred to the colonelcy of the 1st Dragoon Guards. In 1806 the regiment was converted to hussars and in March 1811 was granted the additional title 'Royal', to become the 10th (Prince of Wales's Own Royal) Light Dragoons (Hussars). It served in the Corunna campaign, with especial distinction at Benavente, and returned to the Peninsula with the Hussar Brigade in 1813, serving to the end of the war. It also fought with distinction at Waterloo.

The 10th's regimental distinctions had included yellow facings and silver lace, but the facings were changed to red upon the assumption of the 'Royal' title in March 1811. Also visible here is a lace border around the block of braid loops on the pelisse, a regimental distinction sometimes referred to as 'the frame'. As in the case of other hussar regiments, the 10th adopted shakos: black caps were issued in 1809, and are depicted in Goddard & Booth's *Military Costume of Europe* (1812) and in a watercolour by Denis Dighton of 1813.[1] These were termed 'castor caps' (from the Latin *castor*, a beaver, and by extension something made from beaver-skin), and had no peak. In March 1813, however, when the regiment was at Lisbon, it received new, scarlet, peaked shakos, which were worn also at Waterloo. As usual with hussar regiments which possessed shakos, the fur busbies were reserved for 'dress' occasions. When the regiment was re-clothed in the later part of 1814, their new jackets had blue collar and cuffs. It is curious to note that Hamilton Smith shows the use of the old 'queue' (pigtail), a form of hair-dressing that had been discontinued for the army in general in 1808; but as it is also shown by Dighton, it may have continued in use for some time as a regimental idiosyncracy.

Also distinctive is the rank badge shown in this plate, an inverted chevron worn low upon the sleeve of both jacket and pelisse, with an embroidered Prince of Wales's crest above it (which should not be confused with the design of braid carried above the cuff on officers' jackets, which supposedly imitated the shape of the Prince of Wales's feathers). The wearing of arm-badges by cavalry NCOs seems to have originated in 1801 when the 15th Light Dragoons was granted permission to wear an embroidered crown. Probably subsequent to this the 10th adopted the badge of a Prince of Wales's crest and motto; the Hamilton Smith drawing is probably the earliest illustration showing its use.

Unlike the inverted chevron shown by Hamilton Smith, Dighton depicts chevrons of a more usual style, and a more usual placement, on the upper arm. The use of the Prince of Wales's crest with NCO chevrons continued throughout the regiment's subsequent history, and was discontinued only upon the amalgamation which formed the King's Royal Hussars in 1992.

1. See Sumner, Revd. P., '10th Hussars in Camp on Service, 1813', in *Journal of the Society for Army Historical Research*, Vol. XXIII (1945), p. 156.

A CORPORAL of the 10.TH OR PRINCE of WALES'S OWN ROYAL HUSSARS,

IN REVIEW ORDER.

Plate 16
A Private of the 13th Light Dragoons
(published April 1812)

Raised in 1715, the 13th Dragoons were re-designated as Light Dragoons in 1783, and remained titled as the 13th Light Dragoons, with no supplementary title, until their conversion to hussars in 1861. During the French Revolutionary Wars the regiment saw service in the West Indies, including San Domingo, and in Jamaica during the Maroon War. In early 1810 the regiment went to the Peninsula, joining the army in May of that year and remaining there until the conclusion of the war. The 13th also served with distinction in the Waterloo campaign as part of Arentsschildt's Brigade.

This plate depicts the new light dragoon uniform mentioned in the text to Plate 14; it shows very clearly the facing-coloured piping on the rear seams of the sleeves, which continued down the back of the jacket, and as piping to the pockets on the skirts, also visible here. The 13th's regimental distinctions were buff facings – actually a very pale cream shade – and yellow buttons, hence the yellow lace decoration upon the shako and horse furniture. For parade dress, breeches were worn (buff in the case of the 13th, to match their facings), but overalls were used for other occasions. The 13th had worn blue overalls as early as 1802 (evidently purchased privately as it was remarked in 1804 that the men were still in debt because of them!), but the uniform of 1811–12 included grey overalls, with a double or single stripe of the facing colour (of the regimental lace colour for officers). The new girdle was made of the facing colour, with two blue stripes; for officers the girdle was gold, with two crimson stripes. The shako shown is that described in the text to Plate 14; for active service it might be worn with the plume removed, and with a black waterproof cover; this is shown, for example, in Denis Dighton's print showing Corporal Logan of the 13th killing Colonel Chamorin of the French 26th Dragoons at Campo Mayor in 1811, although Dighton erred in showing the new uniform being worn at so early a date.[1]

Hamilton Smith shows the 'dress' horse furniture in this plate, with the white sheepskin saddle-cover (black for officers), together with the shabraque not generally used on campaign. This bore an edging of the regimental lace and in front and rear corners a device not especially clear in this example of the print: a crown over a reversed 'GR' cypher, over 'XIII' over 'LD'. The valise at the rear of the saddle had matching decoration, bearing in this case 'A' over the 'XIII/LD', the upper letter evidently the troop denomination. The carbine shown here has a covered lock and is attached to the saddle; it might also be attached to the spring-clip upon the private's shoulder belt, which also supported his cartridge-pouch and is shown very well here.

1. This print is illustrated, for example, in Haythornthwaite, P.J., *Wellington's Military Machine*, Tunbridge Wells 1989, p. 19.

A PRIVATE *of the* 13TH LIGHT DRAGOONS.

PLATE 17
An Officer (Lieut[enant] Col[one]l) of the 14th Light Dragoons,
in Parade Dress
(published April 1812)

Raised in 1715 and designated as light dragoons in 1776, the 14th enjoyed an active career during the French wars. A squadron went to Flanders in 1794 and at the end of the campaign was incorporated into the 8th Light Dragoons; in July 1795 the remainder landed at San Domingo, and returned home in October 1797. From December 1808 the regiment served in the Peninsula, collecting the battle honours for Douro, Talavera, Fuentes de Oñoro, Salamanca, Vitoria and Orthez. It returned home in July 1814 but later in the year two squadrons were sent to America and participated in the operations around New Orleans. In 1798 the regiment was granted the title of The Duchess of York's Own (after the Duke's wife, Princess Frederica of Prussia), and was authorised to use the Prussian eagle as a badge, a tradition which extends to the 14th's descendants, the King's Royal Hussars. An acquisition from the Peninsular War was the regimental nickname 'The Emperor's Chambermaids', derived from the 14th's capture at Vitoria of King Joseph Bonaparte's silver chamber-pot, which has graced the regimental mess since that date.

This plate depicts the uniform described in the text to Plate 14, with the 14th's regimental distinctions of orange facings and silver lace, showing how the cap-lines and cockade were gold even for regiments with silver lace. The Dress Regulations of 24 December 1811 noted that officers of light dragoons for parade dress, 'are to wear white leather pantaloons and hussar boots with gold or silver binding according to the lace of their uniform. On ordinary duties or on the march, they are to wear overalls of a colour similar to the private soldier's,' and Sir Thomas Reed, who served at Waterloo with the 12th Light Dragoons, remarked that, 'the buckskin pantaloons with Hessian boots were never worn except upon Church Parade, and we never saw them after Waterloo.'[1] Although white leather belts were worn on service, for dress occasions they were of regimental lace and the facing colour, the pouch belt with silver or gilt mounts of chains and 'pickers' often of a very high degree of workmanship. Plain black leather sabretaches were used by the rank and file, but for officers they had a face of dark blue cloth, edged with gold or silver lace, and bore a crowned, reversed 'GR' cypher over a spray of laurel, in gold, and subsequently came to incorporate regimental symbols.

An item of uniform worn by officers on service but not illustrated by Hamilton Smith was a jacket described in the regulations of December 1811 as 'a short surtout or greatcoat made according to pattern, which is calculated to be worn likewise as a pelisse on service.' It resembled the ordinary jacket in cut and colouring but had facings of 'shag', a fabric with a rough nap; Sir Thomas Reed recalled that at Waterloo the officers of the 12th Light Dragoons wore such a garment, 'a blue cloth pelisse lined with yellow silk plush'. The December 1811 regulations also noted that light dragoon officers attending a drawing room or levée, 'may appear in long coats with lapels and epaulettes, the same as are worn with the jacket, but without lace on the seams; or in the regimental jacket as they may prefer.'

1. Sumner, Revd. P., 'Uniform worn by the 12th Light Dragoons at Waterloo', in *Journal of the Society for Army Historical Research*, Vol. XXV (1947) p. 137.

AN OFFICER (LIEU.^T COL.^L) *of the* 14.TH LIGHT DRAGOONS,

IN PARADE DRESS.

Drawn & Etched by CHS.

Aquatinted by I.C. Stadler.

PLATE 18

A Private of the XVth or King's L[igh]t D[ragoo]ns (Hussars)

(published September 1812)

The 15th was the oldest light cavalry corps, having been raised as light dragoons in 1759, and following its brilliant charges at Emsdorf (1760) was granted the title 'King's'. The regiment won further laurels in Flanders in 1794–95, notably at Villers-en-Cauchies (or 'Villiers-en-Couche' as the battle honour was spelled), and served in North Holland in 1799. From 1807 it was the 15th (or King's) Light Dragoons (Hussars), and in the Corunna campaign won the unique battle-honour 'Sahagun' for another exceptional charge. The regiment returned to the Peninsula in the spring of 1813, served there until the end of the war and fought at Waterloo as part of Grant's Brigade.

The hussar uniform worn by the 15th was like that described in the text to Plates 13 and 15, regimental distinctions including red facings and white metal buttons, and thus white lace, silver for officers. Hamilton Smith depicts three lines of braid above the cuff, a feature shown elsewhere, including by Robert Dighton Jnr.[1]; the regimental pelisse-fur was black, though Dighton shows an NCO with brown fur, presumably a distinction of rank. This illustration shows how the cloth 'bag' rose from the crown of the fur cap; the metal chin-scales were an addition made subsequent to the first issue of the head-dress. Scarlet shakos were ordered for the regiment's 'service' wear, but were not actually taken into use until February/March 1813, while the regiment was in Portugal, en route to the Peninsular army, and the busby seems to have been restored when the regiment returned home. On service grey overalls were worn, for the 15th apparently with a single red stripe.

Also shown here is the full dress shabraque, its decoration consisting of a crown over a scroll (presumably inscribed with the honour 'Emsdorf') over the reversed royal cypher, over crossed flags, the latter representing the French Colours captured at Emsdorf. The man illustrated is shown in course of priming his carbine, ready for skirmishing, which was usually performed by shooting from horseback. The light cavalry carried the short-barrelled 'Paget' carbine, a weapon of no great accuracy, although some regiments – notably the 10th Hussars – were equipped with the very much superior Baker rifled carbine. The furniture of the carbine included a sliding ring upon a bar screwed to the stock, on the opposite side to the lock, with which the gun could be clipped onto the shoulder belt; thus even if dropped during the action, the gun would remain affixed to the soldier's equipment, and would not be lost. The carbine remained clipped to the belt even when it was being used, as is clearly the case here. By mounting the ramrod upon a swivel, which remained attached permanently to the carbine, loss of that vital accoutrement was also prevented.

1. See, for example, Carman, W.Y., '7th, 10th and 15th Hussars 1808–09: Notes on some Water-Colours by Robert Dighton, Junior', in *Journal of the Society for Army Historical Research*, Vol. XXX (1952) pp. 76–80.

A PRIVATE *of the* XV.ᵀᴴ *or* KINGS Lᵀ.Dⁿˢ. (HUSSARS)

PLATE 19
A Private of the 18th Light Dragoons (Hussars)
(published May 1812)

Raised in 1759 as the 19th Light Dragoons and re-numbered as the 18th in 1763, the regiment was converted to hussars in 1807. From 1795 to 1798 it served in the Caribbean, including Jamaica and San Domingo, was in the 1799 campaign in North Holland, and in the Corunna campaign. It returned to the Peninsula in 1813, originally as part of the Hussar Brigade, but in July 1813 was transferred to another brigade. In the Waterloo campaign the 18th served with Vivian's brigade, and Hamilton Smith painted a spirited picture of a charge made by them at Waterloo, showing substantially the same uniform as depicted here, but with plain rather than the indented edging to their shabraques.[1]

Distinctions worn by the 18th included white facings and white-metal buttons; the girdle was blue and white, as just visible here, and the busby brown fur with a light blue bag; unlike the other hussar regiments, the 18th seems never to have adopted a shako. The service overalls were grey, and are depicted as having a single red stripe (a single white stripe in the Hamilton Smith picture of Waterloo mentioned above), and a silver stripe for officers. This illustration shows how the pelisse was worn, slung on one shoulder, but in bad weather it could be worn as a jacket instead (and like other cavalry head-dress, the busby might have a waterproof cover in inclement weather). The pelisse was issued only to hussars; the ordinary light dragoons had no such equivalent, although a painting by Denis Dighton of a member of the 12th Light Dragoons shows a garment similar to the 'surtout' of light dragoon officers, with facings of rough crimson material, but no other reference seems to exist to such garments being worn by the rank and file.[2]

The pointed-ended shabrague with indented (sometimes termed 'Vandycked') lace border was a distinction of the hussar regiments, but generally was used only for 'dress' occasions, in review order. In the Peninsula in February 1813 one of the 18th's officers, Lieutenant George Woodberry, recorded that although the 10th and 15th Hussars had brought their full dress horse-furniture to the campaign, the 18th had not (presumably having only plain shabraques for officers, sheepskins for the other ranks), and that although they could not compete with the other two regiments in terms of appearance, the 18th would look more appropriate for a regiment on campaign.

This plate also shows very clearly the 1796 pattern light cavalry sabre, with its broad, curved blade and stirrup hilt which, as described in the Introduction (p. 15), was the standard armament of all light cavalry from the date of its issue to beyond the end of the Napoleonic Wars.

1. See Haythornthwaite, P.J., *Waterloo Men*, Marlborough 1999, p. 97.
2. See Haswell Miller, A.E., & Dawnay, N.P., *Military Drawings and Paintings in the Royal Collection*, London 1966, Vol. I, fig. 301.

A PRIVATE *of the* 18TH LIGHT DRAGOONS,

(HUSSARS.)

PLATE 20

Light Dragoons serving in the East Indies
[22nd, 8th, 24th; L to R]
(published July 1812)

Senior of the three regiments illustrated serving in the 'East Indies', the 8th Light Dragoons had been raised in 1693 and had borne the title 'The King's Royal Irish' from 1777. After service in Flanders in 1793–94 the regiment served in South Africa, a detachment joining Baird's force in Egypt, and then proceeded to India, where it was distinguished at Leswaree, and returned home in 1822. The 22nd Light Dragoons was raised in 1794 as the 25th, served at the Cape and in India (where it won the battle honour 'Seringapatam'), was re-numbered as the 22nd in 1802, and served in Java in 1811. It was disbanded in 1822. The 24th was raised as the 27th in 1795, served in San Domingo and at the Cape, was re-numbered as the 24th in 1802 and was awarded the badge of an elephant and the honour 'Hindoostan' in commemoration of services under Lake in 1803. It was disbanded in 1818.

Prior to the introduction of the new light dragoon uniform, regiments serving in India had worn a version of the braided light dragoon jacket in 'French grey' – generally a pale blue-grey colour – sometimes with a combed helmet, sometimes styled a 'tin helmet', which was intended to be cooler to wear than the fur-crested 'Tarleton'. (The 8th Light Dragoons had worn such a combed helmet, with a red horsehair mane and a frontal badge of an Irish harp.) With the introduction of the new light dragoon uniform of 1811–12, however, uniform of the ordinary style was worn in the east. The shako of the new pattern was made of drab-coloured felt with tan leather peak and top, but some illustrations of this tropical version of the ordinary head-dress show them in white (as here), rather than in the pale brown shown elsewhere. The horse furniture illustrated here, without the dress shabraque, was the same style as that worn on service in Europe.

The 8th Light Dragoons had red facings and yellow lace, and the 24th light grey facings (shown here with a blue cast) and yellow lace; the facings of the 22nd, however, appear to have presented a problem. They were supposed to wear pink facings and white lace, but when the regiment was inspected at Bangalore in July 1815 it was noted that the officers had been unable to procure cloth of the correct facing colour, so had been permitted to use red facings instead. In the following November, still at Bangalore, although the other ranks were wearing the correct uniform, the officers had still been unable to obtain 'peach blossom cloth', so the problem was resolved by an order which stated that when the next issue of uniforms was made, the regimental facing colour was to be changed to white. (The 21st Light Dragoons appears to have had a similar problem: it was supposed to have pink facings and yellow lace, but was abroad when the new uniform was introduced, and it may be that it had not adopted the pink facings before the regiment was authorised to adopt black facings and white lace in 1814, reverting to yellow lace in June 1815.)

22.th   8.th   24.^d

LIGHT DRAGOONS *Serving in the* EAST INDIES.

PLATE 21
Heavy and Light Cavalry in Watering Order
(published April 1815)

Although the routine might vary due to the conditions of active service, great emphasis was placed upon the well-being of a cavalry regiment's mounts. For example, the 1814 Standing Orders of the 1st Life Guards describe the daily routine: in the morning each horse was to be fed, and then groomed, '1st – Turn round, and the heads and ears well whisped, and ears pulled; they are then to be collared up. 2d – Body well whisped, first against, and then with the grain. 3d – Curried and brushed. 4th – The men to kneel with one knee on the knee-pad, and rub each leg well.' At noon and 4 p.m. the horses were fed again, and in the evening watered, groomed again, and fed.

For these duties the men were equipped with what might be termed a 'working' or 'stable dress', consisting of a single-breasted, tail-less jacket or sleeved, collared waistcoat; Hamilton Smith shows them as red with facing-coloured collar and cuffs for the heavy cavalry, blue with facing-coloured pointed cuffs and a collar patch for the light dragoons. Different details are shown elsewhere: for example, James Howe's painting of the 2nd Dragoons in bivouac in 1815 shows white jackets. A variety of styles of forage cap had been worn for such duty, including folding 'watering caps' or the 'stocking' type, but the style shown by Hamilton Smith seems to have become fairly universal by about 1811, sometimes termed 'Scotch bonnets'. Hamilton Smith shows them as blue, the light dragoon with a facing-coloured band and the heavy cavalryman with white, but there were regimental distinctions. Howe, for example, shows the 2nd Dragoons with blue caps with a red band bearing a yellow zigzag (the zigzag worn to the present day by the successor regiment, the Royal Scots Dragoon Guards), and (appropriately for a Scottish regiment) a red 'toorie' on top. With these garments were worn sturdy stable trousers, often of white 'duck' or canvas.

Officers also possessed undress caps, although these were not regulated officially. For example, William Bragge described one belonging to Lieutenant J.B. Ker of the 9th Light Dragoons, made of blue velvet, with 'gold Tassel and Band of the same edged with white Ermine. How nice.'[1] The degree of latitude permitted in the design of such items may be gauged by a request from the Peninsula made in May 1812 by Captain Thomas Dyneley of the Royal Horse Artillery, quoting Rev. Samuel Wesley in his instructions to the London tailor Hawkes: 'send me out by the next packet a foraging cap from Hawkes. Tell him to let it be much such another as Lieutenant Macdonald of Ross's troop had of him a short time since. If Hawkes does not recollect, send me one "neat but not gaudy".'[2]

---

1. Bragge, W., *Peninsular Portrait 1811–14: The Letters of Captain William Bragge, Third (King's Own) Dragoons*, London 1963, p. 46.
2. Dyneley, T., *Letters Written by Lieut. General Thomas Dyneley, CB, RA, while on Active Service between the Years 1806 and 1815*, ed. Col. F.A. Whinyates, London 1984, p. 23; originally published in *Minutes of Proceedings of the Royal Artillery Institution*, Vol. XXIII, 1896.

HEAVY & LIGHT CAVALRY,
IN WATERING ORDER.

C.H.S

PLATE 22

Heavy and Light Cavalry Cloaked
(published June 1815)

For inclement weather, cavalry were equipped with cloaks sufficiently voluminous to cover the equipment carried on the saddle as well as on the rider. For heavy cavalry the cloaks were made of red cloth, lined with white, with a short cape and a standing collar in the regimental facing colour. For light dragoons the cloak was blue, with a standing collar of the regimental facing colour, and a scarlet lining for officers. The head-dress could be worn similarly with a waterproof cover; this seems to have been quite common for active service in the light dragoons (as quoted in the text for Plate 17, Sir Thomas Reed recalled that oilskin cap-covers were always worn in marching order). Hamilton Smith shows the heavy dragoon wearing the original pattern of helmet (see Plates 9 and 11) with its metal peak and 'caterpillar' crest; and in addition to these, the hussar busby could also be worn with a bad-weather cover.

As shown in Plate 20, the men illustrated here are using the horse furniture appropriate for active service, without the dress shabraque. Beneath the heavy dragoon's cloak can be seen the muzzle of the carbine, inserted into a 'boot' attached to the harness; the end of the pistol-holster is visible alongside, and to the rear of the grain-sack visible behind the rider's right leg is the picket rope.

Cloaks were not worn when action was imminent lest they impeded freedom of movement, yet in the retreat from Quatre Bras to Waterloo, for example, the heavy cavalry is recorded as wearing cloaks. The garment's utility in very bad weather was described by Sergeant Edward Cotton of the 7th Hussars, concerning the night before Waterloo:

> 'Our bivouac was dismal in the extreme; what with the thunder, lightning and rain, it was as bad a night as I ever witnessed, a regular soaker: torrents burst forth from the well-charged clouds upon our comfortless bivouacs, and the uproar of the elements, during the night preceding Waterloo, seemed as the harbinger of the bloody contest. We cloaked, throwing a part over the saddle, holding by the stirrup leather, to steady us if sleepy; to lie down with water running in streams under us was not desirable, and to lie among the horses not altogether safe.'[1]

1. Cotton, E., *A Voice from Waterloo*, 9th edn., Brussels 1900, p. 25.

HEAVY and LIGHT CAVALRY CLOAKED.

PLATE 23

British Cavalry, 1812

(published May 1812)

Hamilton Smith's charts are reasonably self-explanatory, although occasionally variations in colouring may be encountered. The shades of facing colour may not always be exactly that worn by the regiment but are generally a close approximation. The lace colour shown as yellow or white represents gold or silver respectively for officers' distinctions.

The chart for the Life Guards and Royal Horse Guards refers to their lapelled full dress uniforms (see Plate 6) rather than to the subsequent single-breasted jackets; some versions show the breeches of the Royal Horse Guards as buff rather than white. The Dragoon Guards' charts show some of the distinctions between their uniforms and those of the Dragoons: the coloured lines in the girdle and frontal lace are broken rather than of solid colour, and they have red collar patches. Facing colours were blue for the 1st and 4th, black for the 2nd and 7th, white for the 3rd and 6th and green for the 5th; in 1815 the facings of the 3rd changed to blue.

The Dragoon charts show the facings as blue, save for the 4th (green) and 6th (yellow); the other ranks' white lace of the 2nd Dragoons was ordered to be changed to yellow to match their officers' gold lace in October 1811. Shown here is the only gap in the numbered sequence of regiments, the rank between the 4th and 6th Dragoons being unoccupied. The 5th (Royal Irish Dragoons) had been formed in 1689, but having given good service in the 1798 rebellion in Ireland, had enlisted a number of ex-rebels who planned to mutiny and murder their officers. Although only a small number of men were involved, and although it was stated at the time that 'almost every regiment belonging to the Irish establishment, was more or less tainted by the admission of disaffected persons',[1] it was decided to make an example of the regiment and it was disbanded in April 1799, even though it was recognised that such a punishment was unduly harsh. Not until 1858 was a regiment formed again bearing that number, the 5th Royal Irish Lancers; it was thus junior in length of service to the 16th Lancers with which it was amalgamated in 1922, to produce the rather oddly-titled 16th/5th Lancers, the only case in which a higher number preceded a lower in the title of such a regiment.

The Light Dragoon charts include the four regiments of hussars, whose changes in uniform are mentioned in the text to the appropriate plates (by 1815 the 7th and 10th had blue facings and gold lace). Facing colours for the others were: red (8th), crimson (9th, 23rd), pale buff (11th), yellow (12th, 19th), buff (13th), orange (14th, 20th), scarlet (16th), white (17th), pink (21st, 22nd) and light grey (24th, 25th). The problems with the pink facings and the subsequent changes by the 21st and 22nd are detailed in the text to Plate 20.

1. *British Military Library or Journal*, London 1801, Vol. II p. 231.

British Cavalry, 1812.

LIFE GUARDS.

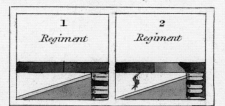

ROYAL HORSE GUARDS.

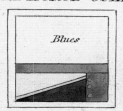

DRAGOON GUARDS.

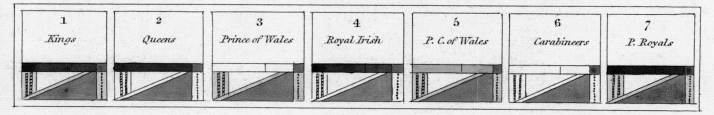

DRAGOONS.

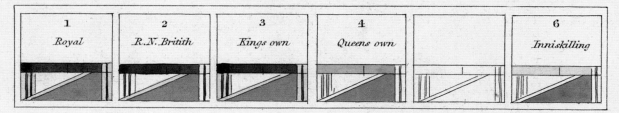

LIGHT DRAGOONS AND HUSSARS.

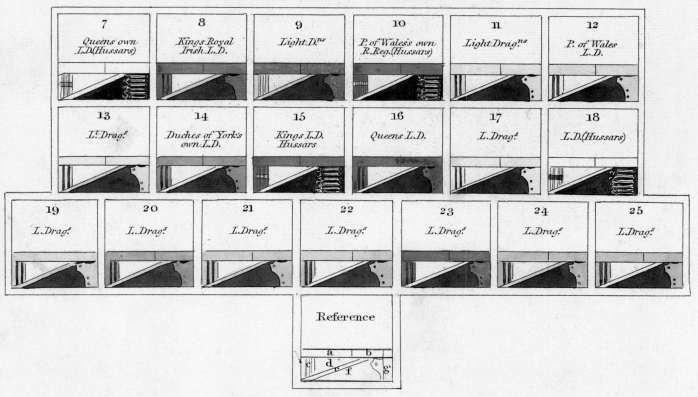

Reference

a Cuff.   e Colour of Officers lace for heavy Dragoons
b Collar.   & Officers & Privates of light Dragoons.
c Sash.   f Colour of Jacket.
d Breeches.   g Lace down the front or lappels.

The Infantry

Plate 24
An Officer of the Guards in Full Dress
(published March 1815)

As noted in the Introduction (p. 16), there were three regiments of Foot Guards at this time: the 1st, 2nd or Coldstream (which rarely used its number) and the 3rd or Scots. The regiment shown here is not specified, but may well be intended to represent the 1st Foot Guards. Then, as now, one of the most obvious ways of distinguishing between their uniforms was in the grouping of their buttons, in singles, pairs and threes respectively.

In addition to the short-skirted jacket introduced for wear on service from 1812, Foot Guards officers had two other styles of coat: a long-tailed coat for full dress, the facings edged with gold lace and the buttons with gold loops, and an undress 'frock' also with long tails and gold lace edging to the facings, but without the button loops. A number of variations is recorded. According to the 1802 draft clothing regulations, both the 'looped' full dress coat and the 'frock uniform coat' should have borne the dark blue facing colour only upon the lapels and cuffs, with the collar scarlet; this does appear in some illustrations, yet Hamilton Smith shows a blue collar, which is also confirmed elsewhere. Instead of the loops shown here, the full dress cuff is usually shown with encircling bands of lace, a narrower band above a wide one, and this is confirmed by extant garments, for example a coat belonging to Lieutenant-Colonel William Miller (mortally wounded at Quatre Bras); furthermore, this has pockets both outlined and covered with lace, rather than the loops shown here. Both the long white gaiters and the cocked hat shown here were worn for reviews or in 'state' dress.

The plate illustrates the voluminous nature of infantry Colours. As noted in the Introduction (p. 19), a regiment of Foot Guards possessed a large number of Colours; for example, when the 1st Guards received a new issue in 1814, the regiment received one standard (bearing the King's cypher), two Colonel's Colours, two Lieutenant-Colonel's, six Major's and 21 Captain's or Company Colours, to which four more were added in 1815. It became the practice for a Colonel's Colour to be associated with the 1st Battalion and a Lieutenant-Colonel's with the 2nd (and in the 1st Guards a Major's with the 3rd Battalion), though this practice was not confirmed officially until 1855. On service each battalion carried only two Colours, probably used in rotation, so that, for example, the 3rd Battalion, 1st Guards at Waterloo carried a crimson Major's Colour and the Union Flag Colour of No. VIII Company, which bore in the centre the company badge, the dragon of Wales. Visible on the Colour shown here is the battle-honour 'Lincelles', awarded to all three Guards regiments on 20 June 1811.

Shown in the background are two regimental bandsmen wearing state clothing, one in a long-tailed, gold-laced coat with black jockey cap, the other in the elaborate, pseudo-oriental clothing worn by musicians of African or Caribbean origin, a very popular fashion for the percussion section of a band and representative of the contemporary popularity for elements of so-called 'Turkish music'.

An OFFICER of the GUARDS in FULL DRESS.

C.H.S.

Aquatinted by I.C.Stadler.

PLATE 25

Grenadiers of the Foot Guards in Full Dress
[2nd, 1st, 3rd; L to R]
(published July 1812)

Illustrated here is the Foot Guards' full dress, with the long white gaiters worn on state occasions. Regimental distinctions are shown clearly: for the 1st Guards, lace loops of 'bastion' shape, spaced singly, and for the 2nd and 3rd Guards, pointed loops in pairs and threes respectively; the lace was white for all three. For the 1st Guards, the rectangular brass shoulder belt plate bore the design of a crowned Garter bearing the motto of that order ('*Honi Soit Qui Mal Y Pense*'), surrounding a reversed 'GR' cypher, with 'III' in the centre. The belt plates of the other regiments were oval: that of the Coldstream Guards bore the eight-pointed star of the Order of the Garter, that of the 3rd Guards the Order of the Thistle, with an oval circlet in the centre inscribed '*Nemo Me Impune Lacessit*', and surrounding a thistle flower. (For officers the belt plates were of a similar design, but executed in gilt for the 1st Guards, gilt with silver and enamel stars for the others.) The brass badges carried upon the other ranks' cartridge boxes bore similar designs, the crowned Garter, Garter Star and Thistle Star respectively, the latter visible on the figure at the right. The men illustrated also exhibit flank company distinctions: facing coloured, laced and fringed wings on the shoulders, instead of the worsted tufted shoulder straps of the ordinary companies, and the white-plumed bearskin cap with white cords, a small brass badge in the form of a flaming grenade at the rear, and a brass plate at the front bearing the royal arms. Such fur caps were worn only by the grenadier companies, and only in full dress – the ordinary shako was the customary wear – and it was this head-dress that was the origin of the bearskin caps worn by the Foot Guards to the present day.

It was announced in the *London Gazette* of 29 July 1815 that henceforth the 1st Guards would be a regiment of grenadiers, styled the First or Grenadier Regiment of Foot Guards, 'in commemoration of their having defeated the Grenadiers of the French Imperial Guards at Waterloo'. This entailed the extension of the use of the grenadier cap to the entire regiment. However, it was not, as often stated, a matter of copying the fur caps of the French troops that they had defeated.

This honour was not appreciated universally; a member of the 1st Guards' light company recalled that:

> 'At Waterloo we lost our green feathers; and when I next joined the company in England, I found them with unwieldy bear-skin caps on their heads. As for myself, being remarkably short, and my cap a very high one, there was nearly as much to be seen above my face as below it; and I looked, for all the world,
>
> > Like Tommy Noddy,
> >
> > All head and no body!
>
> When we were metamorphosed into a grenadier regiment, the light companies requested to be allowed to retain the feather under which they had fought so long: but this was not granted.'[1]

1. 'Green Feather', evidently a nom-de-plume for Charles Parker Ellis, Lieutenant & Captain of the 2nd Battn. at Waterloo, 'Reminiscences of Bayonne', in *United Service Magazine*, 1842, Vol. II, p. 85.

2nd.   1st.   3rd.

GRENADIERS of the FOOT GUARDS.

in full Dress.

Plate 26

Privates of the First Regiment of Foot Guards on Service

(published March 1812)

This plate illustrates a fairly typical infantry uniform for active service, with the distinctions of the 1st Foot Guards: the jacket with blue facings, white lace including loops of 'bastion' shape, spaced singly, and the worsted-tuft-ended shoulder straps of 'battalion' companies.

The head-dress shown is the false-fronted 1812 shako, its design confirmed by a Circular Letter of 18 March 1812. It may have owed the origin of its design to the Portuguese *barretina* cap, or to the old Austrian *casquet*, and it may be found described as the 'Belgic', 'Wellington' or 'Waterloo' shako (the latter because of its use at that battle), but none of these terms was official or contemporary. Made of black felt with a lacquered leather peak, its front was 8¼ in. high and its rear 6¾ in. Its short plume (feathers for officers, worsted for other ranks) was coloured like that of the previous 'stovepipe' shako: white over red for battalion companies, white for grenadiers and green for light companies. Below this was a black cockade secured by a regimental button (sometimes by a grenade or bugle-horn badge for grenadiers and light infantry respectively). Its brass plate was in the form of a crowned rococo shield, normally bearing a reversed 'GR' cypher, though many regimental patterns existed, most commonly bearing the cypher and the regimental number. (For the 1st Guards the badge was a star bearing a Garter surrounding the reversed 'GR', upon the ordinary shield plate; for the 2nd and 3rd Guards the shield bore the stars of the Order of the Garter and Thistle respectively.) In 1814 the plate for light companies was ordered to be replaced by a separate bugle-horn and number, while in the Foot Guards small bugle badges may have been added above the ordinary plate (although a self-portrait of William Payne of the 1st Guards shows a bugle-horn badge worn above a small star, rather than the ordinary shield-plate).[1]

Other ornaments on the shako included the plaited white cords suspended around the front (mixed gold and crimson for officers, often green for light companies), and initially an edging to the false front, worn only by the Guards. The edging is shown here (and the officers' version in a portrait by Edridge of Sir Henry Sullivan of the Coldstream, who was killed at Bayonne, for example), but a War Office letter of 27 June 1812 instructed: 'Gold lace rims of the officers' caps and brass rims on the caps of the soldiers of the three regiments of Foot Guards to be discontinued immediately'; later issues of Hamilton Smith's print had the brass edging painted out. Also shown here is an oilskin 'fall' or neck cover, hooked onto the rear of the shako, which does not appear to have been attached to all caps of this pattern.

The grey service overalls are shown here tucked into black or darker grey gaiters; it is more usual for them to be shown worn outside the gaiters. This also shows the rear of the belts, and the cartridge box badge as described in the text to Plate 25. It was reported in 1802 that although the belts generally used by the line regiments were 2⅛ in. broad, the Guards' bayonet belts were 2¼ in. broad, and their cartridge box belt 2½ in., and that a further distinction was the brass buckles and belt-tips as shown here.

1. Illustrated in Haythornthwaite, P.J., 'A Tale of Two Guardsmen', *Military Illustrated*, No. 14 (1988), p. 30.

CHS

Aquatinted by I.C.Stadler.

PRIVATES *of the* FIRST REGIMENT *of* FOOT GUARDS.

on SERVICE.

Plate 27

Soldiers of the 1st Reg[imen]t of Foot Guards, in Marching Order

(published May 1812)

Although this shows members of the 1st Foot Guards, this plate depicts the general appearance of all infantry in marching order, in cold weather when the greatcoat was worn (see the text to Plate 28). The 1812 shako is shown here with its waterproof cover, with a flap to cover the rear of the neck, and with a separate cover for the plume.

The rear view of the infantry equipment includes a knapsack which is evidently not the type with wood-stiffened sides, but the softer 'envelope' pattern, which is shown by a number of artists as being used by the Foot Guards; the regimental badge painted upon the flap is concealed here by the mess-tin. The private (left) carries his cartridge-box on his right hip and his haversack at the left, over the same shoulder as the bayonet-belt; the haversack was normally made of unbleached canvas but the black version shown here was presumably a regimental pattern. The canteens also appear to be covered with fabric, unlike the wooden canteens which are shown more commonly.

The man at the right is a sergeant; not being armed with a musket, he has no cartridge box, but instead has a sword suspended from the belt over his right shoulder. The tail of his waist-sash can be seen: the 1802 regulations specified that for the 1st Guards these should be crimson with a white stripe, crimson for the Coldstream and striped in crimson, white and blue for the 3rd Guards, but by the date of this plate probably all Foot Guards sergeants had plain crimson sashes, as here. They were also further distinguished by having gold lace on their jackets.

All sergeants except those of light companies carried the half-pike or spontoon, as shown here, a relic of the 'leading staff' carried by officers in the 17th century. Officers' spontoons were discontinued only in April 1786, sergeants carrying halberds until 1792, when they received the spontoons recently relinquished by the officers. It was not a popular weapon – Stephen Morley of the 5th Foot recalled throwing away his at Salamanca, calling it 'a useless piece of furniture',[1] but it was actually used in combat, for example at Waterloo when Sergeant Christopher Switzer of the 32nd Foot speared a French officer who was attempting to grab the Regimental Colour. Another use was recorded by a sergeant of the 1st Foot Guards, who recalled that at Waterloo:

> 'The fight… was so desperate with our battalion, that files upon files were carried out to the rear from the carnage, and the line was held up by the sergeants' pikes placed against the rear – not for want of courage on the men's parts (for they were desperate), only for the moment our loss so unsteadied the line.'[2]

Nevertheless, as one commentator remarked, when sergeants carried pikes instead of muskets, 'the most intelligent and the most expert in the use of arms [were] left totally without the means of defence',[3] a pertinent remark even if a slight exaggeration.

1. Morley, S., *Memoirs of a Serjeant of the 5th Regiment of Foot*, Ashford 1842, p. 114; reprinted Trotman, Cambridge 1999.
2. *United Service Journal*, 1834, Vol. II, pp. 555–56.
3 *Ibid.* 1831, Vol. II, p. 204.

C.H.S. delin.ᵗ

Aquatinted by I.C.Stadler.

SOLDIERS *of the* 1ˢᵗ REGᵗ *of* FOOT GUARDS,

IN MARCHING ORDER.

PLATE 28
Infantry Officer, in Marching Order
(published March 1812)

This, and Plate 30, illustrate the new appearance of infantry officers, following the regulation of 24 December 1811, which stated that they were 'to wear a cap of a pattern similar to that established for the Line', and 'a regimental coat similar to the private men's; but with lapels to button over the breast and body', in place of the previous bicorn hat and long-tailed coat. Also, for regiments serving overseas, 'the Officers are to wear grey pantaloons or overalls, with short boots, or with shoes and gaiters, such as the private men's.'

Prior to this date, the 1802 regulations had described officers' greatcoats as double-breasted, dark blue, with a scarlet falling collar; but from 1811 they were ordered to adopt grey greatcoats as worn by the other ranks, with a standing collar and shoulder-cape. The 1802 regulations had described the other ranks' coats as made of dark grey wool, 'loose made, to come well up about the Neck, have a large Falling Cape to cover the Shoulders, and they are to reach down to (or below) the Calf of the Leg.' From 1811 most sergeants of line regiments had the collar and cuffs of their greatcoats in the regimental facing colour.

Two symbols of commissioned rank are shown here: the crimson waist sash and the gilt metal gorget worn at the neck, engraved with 'GR' and a spray of laurel, a relic of the armoured throat-protection of the 17th century. It was suspended from the upper buttons of the coat by facing coloured rosettes and ribbons (red ribbons for regiments with black facings), but it seems that it was often not worn on campaign. All officers were armed with a sword, those of battalion companies (as shown here) with the 1796 pattern, a straight-bladed weapon designed for thrusting. It had a gilded hilt with a pair of boat-shaped shell-guards, an urn-shaped pommel and a thin knucklebow, and was carried in a gilt-mounted black leather scabbard; its grip was usually bound with silver wire. The gold and crimson sword knot is also illustrated. Officers of grenadier and light companies usually carried the 1803 flank company sabre, a curved-bladed weapon with a knucklebow incorporating the royal cypher, and a lion-head pommel. It was generally carried on slings, whereas the battalion company sword was suspended from a frog. The shoulder belt which supported it, worn beneath the waist sash, usually bore an oval or rectangular plate emblazoned with regimental insignia, frequently (as intended to be shown here) of very superior workmanship. Among the more unusual patterns of belt plate were those worn by officers of the 10th Foot (a silver crescent or gorget-shape, bearing the regimental number) and the 61st Foot (a rectangular silver buckle with a silver slider and belt-tip, the latter bearing 'LXI' and a laurel wreath). Field and some flank company officers might carry the sword suspended from a waist belt.

INFANTRY OFFICER, *in MARCHING ORDER.*

C.H.S.

Aquatinted by I.C.Stadler.

PLATE 29

Battalion Infantry: 6th, or 1st Warwickshire Regiment;
23rd, or Royal Welsh Fusileers [R to L]
(published February 1815)

In this plate two line regiments are illustrated. Raised for Dutch service in 1673, the 6th Regiment of Foot received its county affiliation as the 1st Warwickshire Regiment in 1782. During the early Revolutionary Wars it served in the Caribbean, including at Martinique and Guadeloupe, in Ireland 1796–98 and in Canada 1799–1806. In 1803 a 2nd Battalion was formed, which remained at home; the 1st Battalion served in the early Peninsular War (Roliça, Vimeiro and the Corunna campaign), and at Walcheren. In November 1812 it rejoined the Peninsular army and served in the 7th Division for the remainder of the war, including Vitoria, the Pyrenees, Nivelle and Orthez, all of which it received as battle honours, and then served in America, winning the honour 'Niagara'. It returned to Europe too late for the Waterloo campaign, but served in the army of occupation in France.

The 23rd Regiment was formed in 1689 by the regimentation of some existing independent companies; its title of Royal Welsh Fusileers (sic: now normally spelled 'Welch Fusiliers', but 'Fuzileers' also used in *Army List* of the time) originated in 1714. It served in San Domingo, in the expedition to North Holland in 1799, and in Egypt. A 2nd Battalion was formed and served in the Corunna and Walcheren campaigns, but the 1st Battalion's service was more extensive, including Copenhagen (1807), Martinique (1809) and from July 1810 in the Peninsula, originally with the 1st Division but from that October with the 4th, perhaps most notably at Albuera, though it won eight other Peninsular battle honours. It also fought at Waterloo.

Shown here is the classic appearance of the infantry following the introduction of the single-breasted coat, without lapels, in 1797, with short skirts and which became slightly shorter at the waist in the early 1800s. Regimental distinctions included the collar, cuffs and shoulder straps in the facing colour, and white lace with an interwoven design and a variety of loopings on the button holes. For the 6th the facings were deep yellow, the lace square-ended, in pairs, with red and yellow stripes; for the 23rd, blue facings, 'bastion' shaped loops and lace with red, blue and yellow stripes. Fusilier regiments wore the shoulder wings which were otherwise the preserve of flank companies, and in full dress a fur cap with brass plate, peak, white cords and plume. The 1802 regulations described this as similar to the cap worn by grenadiers, but not so high, and without the grenade badge on the rear. For ordinary occasions, fusiliers wore the shako.

For the 6th, at least two designs of other ranks' shoulder belt plate are recorded, both oval; one had a crown over '6', with '1st Warwickshire' above and 'Regiment' below; the other 'VI' surrounded by 'First Warwickshire Regiment of Foot'. The 23rd had worn oval plates bearing the Prince of Wales's crest over '23', but Hamilton Smith shows what is apparently a later pattern, perhaps an other ranks' version of the officers' rectangular plate which bore the Prince of Wales's crest over 'XXIII' within a crowned strap bearing the regimental title. Both men wear grey overalls and short gaiters, as used on active service.

BATTALION INFANTRY,
6TH or 1ST WARWICKSHIRE REGIMENT,
23RD or ROYAL WELSH FUSILEERS.

PLATE 30

IXth or E[ast] Norfolk Regiment of Infantry: An Ensign
Bearing the Regimental Colours, & A Colour Serjeant on Service
(published December 1813)

Raised in 1685, the 9th Foot bore the territorial affiliation of East Norfolk. At the beginning of the French Revolutionary Wars it was in the Caribbean, where it remained until 1796. Enlarged to three battalions – the two junior were disbanded at the Peace of Amiens – it served in North Holland in 1799 and briefly in Portugal. The 1st Battalion served in the expedition to Hanover in 1805, in the early Peninsular War (including Roliça), at Walcheren, and returned to the Peninsula in April 1810. From August of that year it served in the 5th Division, including the battles of Busaco, Salamanca, Vitoria, San Sebastian and Nive. At the end of the war it went to Canada, returning home in August 1815. A re-formed 2nd Battalion served at Vimeiro and Corunna, left Wellesley's army in June 1809, and fought subsequently in the southern part of the Peninsular War, including at Barrosa, Tarifa and Tarragona. It returned home in 1813 and was disbanded in December 1815.

This plate shows the infantry officers' uniform decreed in December 1811 (see the text to Plate 28), including the short-tailed, double-breasted jacket with collar, cuffs and lapels (which might be turned back all or part way) in the facing colour (yellow for the 9th), and in some cases lace loops in the button colour (silver for the 9th). Regiments with buff facings had turnbacks of the same colour, as shown here, though for a yellow-faced regiment white turnbacks would have been expected. The ensign wears grey breeches tucked into Hessian boots, an alternative for officers to the overall trousers. He carries the Regimental Colour half-furled, easier to handle in battle; the belt for its support is carried over the left shoulder.

The Colour is protected by a colour-sergeant armed with a spontoon; like the ensign he is a member of a battalion company (white-over-red plume and tufted shoulder straps). The rank of colour-sergeant was instituted in July 1813 as a reward of merit for one sergeant in every company; instead of the usual three chevrons, its rank badge upon the right upper arm was a crown over a Union Flag, over crossed swords, over a single chevron. As a sergeant he wears a crimson waist-sash with a facing-coloured central stripe, and white lace (the lace of the 9th's other ranks was in pairs, with two black stripes). He wears the standard infantry equipment, including a light blue wooden canteen and unbleached canvas haversack.

The 9th's regimental device, displayed here upon the shoulder belt plates and the Colour, was the figure of Britannia, which appears to have been awarded to the regiment following the War of the Spanish Succession. The belt plates were oblong, bearing a seated Britannia with laurel branch, spear and 'Union' shield, upon a tablet inscribed 'IX Regt.' Various versions are recorded for officers, including that shown, with a silver device mounted on gilt, though as a silver-laced regiment silver plates would have been more usual. The significance of the figure of Britannia is said to have escaped some of the inhabitants of the Peninsula, who took it to represent the Virgin Mary; hence the regimental nickname 'the Holy Boys'!

Aquatinted by I.C.Stadler.

IX.ᵀᴴ ᴏʀ E.NORFOLK REGIMENT ᴏғ INFANTRY.

An ENSIGN bearing the REGIMENTAL COLOURS.

& A COLOUR SERJEANT on SERVICE.

PLATE 31

Grenadiers [L] & Light Infantry of the 29th
or Worcestershire Regiment of Infantry on Duty at Home

(published May 1813)

Raised in 1694, the 29th served as marines aboard the fleet in the early Revolutionary Wars – a detachment was present at the Battle of the 'Glorious First of June' – and was then ordered to the West Indies. Amalgamated with a newly-raised 2nd Battalion when it returned home, it was in Ireland in 1798, North Holland in 1799 and Canada 1802–07. It went to the Peninsula in 1808 and was the last regiment to fight a battle (Roliça) wearing the old-style hair-dressing of queue and powder. It served in the Peninsula until 1811, notably at Albuera, and suffered so heavily that it was sent home to recruit (October 1811). Wellington described it as 'the best regiment in the army, has an admirable internal system, and excellent non-commissioned officers',[1] but lamented its lack of a 2nd Battalion to supply reinforcements.

Moyle Sherer saw the regiment at about the same time and left a memorable description:

'Nothing could possibly be worse than their clothing; it had become necessary to patch it; and as red cloth could not be procured, grey, white and even brown had been used: yet, under this striking disadvantage, they could not be viewed by a soldier without admiration. The perfect order and cleanliness of their arms and appointments, their steadiness on parade, their erect carriage, and their firm and free marching, exceeded any thing of the kind which I had seen. No corps of any army or nation, which I have since had an opportunity of seeing, has come nearer to my idea of what a regiment of infantry should be, than the old twenty-ninth.'[2]

The regiment returned to the Peninsula in 1813, where service at Cadiz and Gibraltar was followed by transfer to North America, from where it returned just too late for the Waterloo campaign.

This plate shows the uniform of flank companies on home service, where breeches and gaiters were worn in place of overalls. Flank company distinctions are shown in the shoulder-wings and distinctive head-dress, including the grenadier cap (which had the regimental device set upon a cloth patch at the top rear, with a small metal grenade badge below), and the 1812 shako with green light company plume (but minus its cords). The 29th had yellow facings and lace loops in pairs, the lace with one yellow and two blue stripes. Plate 37 shows square-ended loops with two blue stripes, whereas this plate has pointed loops which are almost certainly correct.

The belt plates bear the regimental number with an inscription above, presumably 'Roleia' (the early spelling of the battle honour 'Roliça'), which is known to have been carried upon other accoutrements, and is probably what is borne above the '29' and laurel wreath on the knapsack. The grenadier (on the left) carries a brass match-case on his shoulder belt, a piece of equipment redundant since grenades had ceased to be carried in the early 18th century, but retained as a symbol of grenadiers, while the light company man wears a non-regulation waist belt, probably made from a musket-sling, which was adopted by some regiments as a way of holding the equipment in place, especially necessary for the more active movements of light infantry. It is possible that the background here is intended to represent Windsor, where the 29th was stationed in 1812.

1. Gurwood, J., ed., *Dispatches of Field-Marshal the Duke of Wellington*, London 1834–38, Vol. V, p. 146; entry for 12 September 1809.
2. Sherer, M., *Recollections of the Peninsula*, London 1825, pp. 84–85; reprinted with Introduction by P.J. Haythornthwaite, Spellmount, Staplehurst 1996.

GRENADIERS & LIGHT INFANTRY
OF THE 29TH OR WORCESTERSHIRE REGIMENT OF INFANTRY
ON DUTY AT HOME.

PLATE 32
Grenadiers of the XLIId or Royal and XCIId or Gordon Highlanders [L to R]
(published September 1812)

The original and most senior of the Highland corps, the 42nd Royal Highland Regiment (Black Watch) had been formed in 1739 from independent companies. In the French Revolutionary Wars it had served in Flanders, in the West Indies 1796–97, and notably in Egypt in 1801. A 2nd Battalion was formed in July 1803. The 1st Battalion went to Gibraltar in 1805 and from there to the Peninsula, serving at Roliça, Vimeiro and Corunna, and subsequently at Walcheren. The 2nd Battalion joined the 1st Division of Wellington's army after Talavera and served until May 1812, when it drafted most of its men to the 1st Battalion which replaced it, transferring to the 6th Division in November 1812 in which it remained for the rest of the war. In all the regiment won eight Peninsular battle honours.

The 92nd Highland Regiment was raised as the 100th in 1794 by the family of the Duke of Gordon (hence the regimental title), served in the Mediterranean and Ireland and was re-numbered as the 92nd in 1799. It served in North Holland, Egypt, at Copenhagen, Corunna and Walcheren, returning to the Peninsula in October 1810, joining the 1st Division. In June 1811 it transferred to the 2nd Division, with which the regiment remained for the remainder of the war, winning eight battle honours. Both the 42nd and 92nd served with distinction in the Waterloo campaign, notably at Quatre Bras.

Highland uniform was very distinctive. Their jackets were like those of the ordinary infantry, but the 1802 regulations noted that they had but eight loops on the breast, and diagonal pockets like the light infantry rather than horizontal. The head-dress was the Highland bonnet with diced band, decorated with black feathers and which could be worn with a peak attached. The bulky 'belted plaid' (*breachan-an-fhéilidh*) of the late 18th century had given way to the 'little kilt' (*philabeg*); the sporran was not worn on campaign. On campaign officers generally wore breeches or trousers, as did those other ranks whose kilts had worn out if replacements were unavailable. Officers' and sergeants' sashes were worn over the left shoulder, and these ranks carried basket-hilted broadswords of the type shown at the feet of the men illustrated. As grenadiers, both men wear shoulder-wings and white plumes. The 42nd had blue facings and bastion loops, spaced singly, with a red stripe. Traditionally, the 42nd wore red plumes from at least the 1790s (the circumstances of its origin are stated variously), which are shown on the figures in the background. Although the corporal shown has a white plume, some sources suggest that the grenadiers' plume was white with a red tip, and the light company plume green with a red tip.

From its inception the regiment wore a dark tartan – one explanation for the name 'Black Watch' – which became known by that title, or officially as the 'government' sett. It seems that at one time a red stripe was included in it, probably just for the grenadiers, as shown here, although it may have been worn by the rest at some time. The 92nd had yellow facings, loops in pairs and bearing a blue stripe, and a kilt of Gordon tartan, the 'government' sett with a yellow overstripe.

GRENADIERS *of the* XLII. *or* ROYAL, *and* XCII. *or*

GORDON HIGHLANDERS.

London Pub.d Sep.t 1.st 1812 by Colnaghi & Co. 23 Cockspur Street.

PLATE 33

An Officer & Private of the 52d Reg[imen]t of L[igh]t Infantry

(published November 1814)

Raised in 1755 as the 54th, and renumbered in 1757, the 52nd Regiment received the territorial affiliation of 'Oxfordshire' in 1782. In India at the beginning of the French Wars, it came home in 1798 and was converted to light infantry in 1803. As described in the Introduction (p. 17), Sir John Moore made it a model for the army, not only in the perfection of light infantry tactics (much of which were developed from existing ideas) but perhaps more importantly in his concept of leadership and *esprit de corps*, arising from humane treatment of the other ranks. By teaching the officers until:

> 'They became perfectly acquainted with the system, they could teach the men, and by their zeal, knowledge, and, above all, good temper and kind treatment of the soldier, make the regiment the best in the service; and… it did become the finest and best behaved corps, both as regard officers and men, that was ever seen; and… was considered a model for the rest of the army.'[1]

The 52nd was trained by Moore at the camp at Shorncliffe, alongside the 43rd Light Infantry and 95th Rifles, which regiments later formed the nucleus of the élite Light Division of the Peninsular army.

The 1st Battalion 52nd arrived in the Peninsula in 1809 and served there for the remainder of the war, generally in the forefront of the action with the Light Division, and earned thirteen battle honours. The 2nd Battalion, raised in 1804, joined the Light Division in March 1811 but was drafted into the 1st Battalion in February 1812; it also served in the Netherlands in 1813–14. The 1st Battalion 52nd, commanded by Sir John Colborne (1778–1863, later Field Marshal Lord Seaton), one of the best battalion commanders in the army, served in the 1815 campaign and executed the vital manoeuvre that helped defeat Napoleon's last attack by the Imperial Guard at Waterloo.

Light infantry regiments wore the basic infantry uniform, all having shoulder wings, but they never adopted the 1812 shako, retaining the light infantry version of the previous cylindrical or 'stovepipe' shako, with a frontal green plume and a bugle-horn badge. (The 71st Light Infantry wore the blue Highland bonnet with diced band blocked into the shape of a shako.) The 52nd had buff facings (note here the buff turnbacks, as worn by buff-faced regiments; their breeches were also buff), the lace in pairs, with a red stripe, and silver lace for officers. The officer illustrated wears the light infantry version of the waist sash, with cords instead of the usual hanging tails, has silver-fringed wings, and carries the regimental pattern of sabre, which had a stirrup hilt similar to that of the 1796 light cavalry pattern. Both the belt plates illustrated bear just the regimental number '52', the officer's plate silver and the private's brass, although other patterns are recorded for officers, one having the number within a crowned strap inscribed 'Oxfordshire Regiment'. As evidence of Sir John Moore's concern for his regiment, it is recorded that he obtained shoulder belts one half-inch wider than the regulation, these being more comfortable to wear, and which were copied subsequently by other regiments. The soldiers illustrated are advancing with muskets at the trail, a position commonly used by light infantry.

---

1. Napier, Sir George, *Passages in the Early Military Life of Sir George T. Napier, KCB*, ed. W.C.E. Napier, London 1884, p. 13.

_An_ OFFICER & PRIVATE _of the_ 52ª _REGᵗ of LᵗINFANTRY._

PLATE 34

British Riflemen
[60th Regt., 95th Regt.; L to R]
(published May 1813)

As described in the Introduction (p. 18), the 5th Battalion, 60th (Royal American) Regiment was the first battalion in the army to be armed exclusively with rifles, and the first regular battalion to wear green uniforms. (The senior, 'line' battalions of the 60th mainly wore ordinary infantry uniform in red, with blue facings, and lace with two blue stripes, the loops in pairs; their rifle companies, and the whole of the regiment's 7th and 8th Battalions, raised in 1813, wore green.) The 5th Battalion served throughout the Peninsular War, its companies generally dispersed among the various divisions, to give each an enhanced skirmishing facility. The battalion remained largely 'foreign' in composition, principally German, throughout. As illustrated here its uniform included the light infantry shako with green cords and plume, green jacket with scarlet facings and three rows of buttons on the breast, blue breeches with scarlet piping, and black leather equipment.

The Introduction also describes the origin of the 95th or Rifle Regiment, arguably the most famous unit in the army, with matchless *esprit de corps* exemplified by the large number of personal accounts of the Peninsular War that were published by its members, one reason for the unit's subsequent fame. The 95th's supreme skill was described most effectively by an experienced officer of the Portuguese Caçadores, concerning an action near Tarbes in 1814:

> 'Nothing could exceed the manner in which the ninety-fifth set about the business... Certainly I never saw such skirmishers... They could do the work much better and with infinitely less loss than any other of our best light troops. They possessed an individual boldness, a natural understanding, and a quickness of eye, in taking advantage of the ground, which, taken altogether, I never saw equalled. They were, in fact, as much superior to the French voltigeurs, as the latter were to our skirmishers in general.'[1]

The regiment's uniform was distinctive: light infantry shako with green plume and cords (and often shown with a bugle-horn badge, absent here); dark green jacket with black facings and white piping, with three rows of buttons on the breast; dark green trousers, and equipment of black leather throughout; altogether a sombre aspect which gave rise to the regimental nickname, 'the Sweeps'. Officers wore braided jackets of hussar style, and increased the light cavalry appearance of their costume by wearing pelisses at times.

The standard rifle, carried by both men shown here, was that designed by Ezekiel Baker and bearing his name. The Baker Rifle had a 30-inch barrel and a calibre generally of 0.625 in. ('carbine bore'; ordinary 'musket bore' was about 0.75 in.). It was capable of great feats of accuracy, and could use either 'prepared cartridges' (like those used for the ordinary musket), which maximised the rate of fire, or could be loaded with loose powder and ball, for maximum accuracy. The powder was carried in powder horns, as being used by the 60th man in this plate, and the loose balls usually in a small pouch by the waist belt clasp, as carried by the 95th man here. The Baker rifle had a bayonet with a 23-inch 'sword' blade, and a brass hilt and knucklebow, although unaccountably this plate shows a sword-bayonet without a knucklebow.

---

1. Blakison, J., *Twelve Years' Military Adventures in Three Quarters of the Globe*, London 1829.

60.th Rg.^t   95.th Rg.^t

BRITISH RIFLEMEN.

A Sergeant and Privates of the 87th, or Prince of Wales's Own
Irish Regiment on Service

(published January 1813)

In this plate Hamilton Smith combines the new uniform with an earlier incident, to form an impossible combination but one which would have been familiar to all contemporary observers. The 87th was formed in 1793 as the Prince of Wales's Irish Regiment. Its 1st Battalion served in Flanders 1794–95, in the Caribbean, South America, at the Cape and in Mauritius until 1815, when it proceeded to India. Its 2nd Battalion, raised in Ireland in 1804, went to the Peninsula and served at Talavera with the 3rd Division. In 1810 it joined Graham at Cadiz and at Barrosa (5 March 1811) Sergeant Patrick Masterson captured the Eagle of the French 8th Line Regiment, the first to be taken in combat during the war. This – the event commemorated in the plate – was so celebrated that the regiment was granted the title 'Prince of Wales's Own' and the right to use an eagle as a badge. Subsequently the 2nd Battalion served at Tarifa, and in October 1812 joined Wellington's 3rd Division, with which it served for the remainder of the war.

Denis Dighton produced a print of Masterson's capture of the Eagle, showing the uniform worn at the time (including the 'stovepipe' shako); conversely, Hamilton Smith refers to the incident here, while showing the 1812 uniform and in the background the Regimental Colour decorated with the eagle symbol awarded for the feat. The devices on the Colour include the Prince of Wales's feathers backed by a sunburst, over an eagle, over a harp, over '87', these devices surrounded by a 'Union' wreath (roses, thistles and shamrock), with a scroll below inscribed 'Prince/of Wales's Own/Irish'.

Regimental facings were green, the lace with a red stripe and loops in pairs. Sergeants in general were distinguished by scarlet jackets, at least when new notably different from the duller red worn by the lower ranks, by white lace, and the sash with facing-coloured stripe. Curiously, the sergeant illustrated here has his three rank chevrons inverted. This may have been a regimental idiosyncracy, and it was perhaps by following this print that Louis Lejeune showed the same detail in his painting of Barrosa, which also shows the wrong shako for the date. The eagle over harp insignia is visible upon the sergeant's shako plate. Illustrated here is the sergeants' pattern of sword (similar to the officers' 1796 model), and at the left, the rear of the infantry equipment, with rather unusual dark-coloured haversacks and canteens, as shown in Plate 27. Like the sergeant, the man ramming a charge down the barrel of his musket (left) belongs to a battalion company (white over red plume); the private at the right is a member of the light company (shoulder-wings and green plume; curiously, no shako cords are shown).

A number of patterns of belt plate are recorded for this regiment, the oval one for this period probably that bearing the Prince of Wales's crest over a harp over '87', but a subsequent pattern, including the eagle, honour 'Barrosa' and the new title 'Prince of Wales's Own' was oblong, and worn by officers; perhaps a corresponding other ranks' pattern is that worn by the light company man. The portrayal of the captured Eagle has two faults: the sculpted bronze eagle itself is too small, and the inscription upon the flag incorrectly identifies the regiment as the 8th Light Infantry.

CH.S.

Aquatinted by I.C.Stadler.

A SERGEANT AND PRIVATES OF THE 87.TH

OR PRINCE of WALES'S OWN IRISH REGIMENT on SERVICE.

PLATE 36
Drum Major &c. of a Regiment of the Line,
Pioneer of the Grenadier Comp[an]y of D[itt]o
(published March 1815)

The significance of regimental musicians and drummers is noted in the Introduction (p. 19). It was usual to dress a regimental band in very elaborate uniforms – white uniforms with coloured facings were popular – but the traditional dress of the drummers (and fifers) was so-called 'reversed colours': the body of their coat in the regimental facing colour, and their facings red, as here, with elaborate lacing on the seams and chevrons on the sleeves. (Drummers of 'royal' regiments, those with blue facings, did not usually wear 'reversed colours'.) Such uniforms made the drummers and musicians very conspicuous to the enemy, however, and a General Order of 25 September 1811 stated that because their loss in action 'may be ascribed to the marked difference of their dress, their clothing may be of the same colour as that worn by their respective regiments', with distinctions just in the lace; but the order seems somewhat ambiguous and does not seem to have been obeyed universally.

Drummers might wear bearskin caps in full dress, but usually wore shakos on service. The drummer and fifer shown – the latter has a long, brass fife-case hanging by his right thigh – appear to be boys, although the traditional image of the 'drummer boy' is an exaggeration, and many drummers were mature men. As illustrated, the drums generally had wooden bodies, and bore painted devices (usually the regimental identification) upon a facing-coloured ground; the diagonally striped red and white hoops seem to have been a quite common design. Drum-majors, who usually ranked as sergeants, often wore magnificent uniforms including features normally restricted to officers – metallic lace, epaulettes and, as illustrated, a long-tailed coat similar in cut to that worn by officers prior to the introduction of the short-tailed jacket. The facing-coloured baldric with metallic lace decoration, and bearing two drumsticks, and the silver-mounted mace, were traditional items of drum-major's equipment.

The men of a battalion's pioneer section were the only other ranks permitted to grow beards. Their equipment included a variety of tools appropriate to the manual tasks and field fortifications that they undertook: saws, billhooks, mattocks, spades and, as here, the felling-axe carried in a leather sheath over the right shoulder, which apart from its utility became a traditional symbol of the role of pioneer, as did the leather apron. Their head-dress was a fur cap, the plate (as here) bearing symbols of their duties (here a crossed saw and axe); the 1802 regulations prescribed these symbols and the king's crest upon a red ground, and for drummers' cap plates the crest, drums and trophies of colours upon a black ground, but as in the case of grenadiers' caps, all-brass plates are found in illustrations.

Although the regiment shown is not identified, it has been speculated that it represents the 66th (Berkshire) Regiment.[1] Its facings were described variously as yellowish, light or pea green, or as the brownish-green shade known as 'gosling green'; its lace bore crimson and green and crimson stripes, and its loops were spaced singly. The regiment's 1st Battalion went to Ceylon in 1806 and from there to India; the 2nd Battalion, formed in 1803, served in the Peninsula from 1809 and won nine battle honours. When the battalions amalgamated, the 66th helped provide the guard on St Helena during Napoleon's captivity there.

1. See Sumner, Revd. P., 'Drum-Major and Pioneer, 66th Foot, 1815', in *Journal of the Society for Army Historical Research*, Vol. XXII (1943), p. 131.

C.H.S.

Aquatinted by I.C.Stadler.

DRUM MAJOR &c. of A REGIMENT of the LINE.

PIONEER of the GRENADIER COMPᵞ of Dᵒ.

PLATE 37
British Infantry of the Line, 1812

Unlike the cavalry chart (Plate 23), no key is provided for Plates 37 or 38 on which appear the infantry regiments, but each regimental block is easily comprehensible. The upper section states the number, title (sometimes abbreviated: see Appendix 1, page 172, for full versions) and the number of battalions maintained by the regiment in 1812. (Those not specified were single-battalion regiments.) Below these details, the coloured horizontal bar represents the regimental facing colour, and below that are two triangles formed by the inclusion of a diagonal bar. The upper triangle shows the colour of the breeches (or kilt) with at the far left the coloured design woven into the regimental lace; evidently the left-hand edge of the strip represents the 'inside' edge of the lace loops, the right-hand side the 'outside' (see the Introduction pp. 36–37 for more details of lace design). The diagonal bar (yellow or white) represents the officers' lace (gold or silver respectively); the lower red triangle represents the jacket, the white shapes showing the design of lace loop, square-ended or 'bastion', evenly-spaced or in pairs (threes for the 3rd Foot Guards).

The following details concern the facing colours, and refer both to this plate and to the charts in Plate 38. Facings were sometimes described with nuances of shade which were not always constant. Some are included in the 1802 regulations, for example, from which some of the following descriptions have been taken. The 'royal' regiments with blue facings were the 1st, 2nd, 4th, 7th, 8th, 18th, 21st, 23rd, 25th, 42nd, 60th and 97th. A number of shades of yellow are recorded; those with facings described as just 'yellow' were the 9th, 12th, 15th, 16th, 29th, 37th, 38th, 44th, 57th, 77th, 80th, 82nd–86th, 91st–93rd and 102nd, plus the 46th which is also described as wearing pale yellow, and the 72nd, 'yolk'. Pale yellow facings included the 20th, 26th, 30th, 67th, 88th and 99th; 'deep yellow' the 6th, 75th and 100th; 'bright yellow' the 10th, 28th and 34th; and 'philemot yellow' (*feuille-mort*, dead-leaf colour) the 13th. Buff facings were worn by the 3rd, 14th, 27th, 31st, 40th, 48th, 52nd, 61st, 71st, 78th, 81st, 96th, 98th, 103rd and 104th, with 'pale buff' described for the 22nd, 'yellowish buff' for the 62nd and 'deep buff' for the 90th (regiments with buff facings were supposed to wear matching buff breeches and leather equipment). Facings of 'gosling green' (a brownish shade) were worn by the 5th; 'full green' by the 11th and 49th; 'deep green' by the 19th, 45th and 68th; 'very deep green' by the 63rd; 'dark green' by the 55th, 73rd and 79th; 'willow green' by the 24th and 69th, and 'popinjay green' by the 54th. The 39th's facings were described as either green or 'pea green', the 51st's 'deep green', later 'grass green', the 36th and 66th as either 'yellowish' or 'gosling' green, and the 87th and 94th wore an unspecified shade of green. White facings were worn by the 32nd, 43rd, 47th, 59th, 65th, 74th and 101st, and 'greyish white' by the 17th. Red facings were worn by the 33rd, 41st, 53rd and 76th, black by the 50th, 58th, 64th, 70th and 89th, orange by the 35th and purple by the 56th. In addition to the possibility that the exact shade of facing colour may not have remained entirely constant over the years, occasionally facing colours were changed: the 25th (Sussex) Regiment changed its deep yellow facings to blue in 1805, when it became a 'royal' regiment as the King's Own Borderers, and the 86th changed from the yellow shown here to blue in 1812.

BRITISH INFANTRY OF THE LINE
1812
FOOT GUARDS

1st Regiment 3 battalions	2d Rt or Coldstream 2 battalions	3d Regiment 2 battalions

NUMBERED REGIMENTS OF FOOT

1st or Royal Scots 4 batts.	2d or Quees Royal	3d Et Kent or buffs 2 batts.	4th or King's own 2 batts.	5th Northumberland 2 batts.	6th 1st Warwickshire 2 batts.	7th Royal Fuziliers 2 batts.	8th or the King's 2 batts.
9th East Norfolk 2 batts.	10th North Lincoln 2 batts.	11th North Devon 2 batts.	12th East Suffolk 2 batts.	13th First Somerset	14th Buckingham 2 batts.	15th York E. Riding 2 batts.	16th Bedfordshire
17th Leicestershire	18th Royal Irish 2 batts	19th 1st York N. Riding	20th East Devons.	21st R.N. British Fuz. 2 batts	22d Cheshire	23d Royl Welsh Fuzil. 2 batts.	24th Warwickshire 2 batts.
25th King's Own Border. 2 batts.	26th Cameronian 2 batts.	27th Inniskilling 3 batts	28th N. Gloucester 2 batts.	29th Worcestershire	30th Cambridgeshire 2 batts.	31st Huntindonshe. 2 batts.	32d Cornwall 2 batts.
33d 1st Y.W. Riding	34th Cumberland 2 batts.	35th Sussex 2 batts.	36th Herefordshire 2 batts.	37th N. Hampshire	38th 1st Staffordshire 2 batts.	39th Dorsetshire 2 batts.	40th 2d Somerset
41st 2 batts.	42d Royal Highd. 2 batts.	43d Monmouth L.Infy. 2 batts.	44th East Essex 2 batts.	45th Nottingham 2 batts.	46th S. Devon	47th Lancashire 2 batts.	48th Northampton 2. batts.
49th Hertfordshire	50th W. Kent 2 batts.	51st 2d Yk W. Ridg L.Inf.	52d Oxfordshire L Infy. 2 batts.	53d Shropshire 2 batts.	54th W. Norfolk	55th Westmoreland	56th W. Essex 2 batts.
57th W. Middlesex 2 batts.	58th Rutland 2 batts.	59th 2nd Nottingham 2 batts.	60th Royal American 6 batts.	61st S. Gloucester 2 batts.	62d Wiltshire 2 batts.	63d W. Suffolk 2 batts.	64th 2d Staffordshire
65th 2d York North Riding	66th Berkshire 2 batts	67th S. Hampshire 2 batts	68th Durham Light Infr	69th S. Lincoln 2 batts	70th Surry	71st Highland L.Infy 2 batts	72d 2 batts

Plate 38
Regular Infantry Continued, Royal Artillery

This plate continues the coverage of the infantry begun in Plate 37, and illustrates some other units, in addition to the section on the Royal Artillery. Notes involving the infantry facing colours are given in the text to Plate 37, and some additional comments on regimental laces also appear in the Introduction (pp. 36–37).

Just as some of the facing colours shown in these charts may not always be an exact match to the descriptions of shades recorded elsewhere, so some designs of other ranks' lace do not conform with other sources; indeed, variations are not unknown in other versions of the same charts. Nevertheless, the Hamilton Smith charts represent an important primary source for these details. Sometimes it is difficult to differentiate between blue and black stripes, for example, or between red and the crimson stripe used by the 15th. A dotted line represents an interwoven two-coloured line or 'worm': yellow and black for the 15th, black and white for the 32nd, blue and yellow for the 34th, for example. In this particular version of the chart, some laces are left uncoloured. According to the 1802 regulations their lace design was: 13th, yellow stripe; 14th, pale yellowish-buff stripe on one edge, blue and red worm on the other; 45th, green stripe; 61st, blue stripe on outside edge; 62nd, two blue and one straw-coloured stripes. In some cases the colouring of the kilt in Plate 37 has incorrectly covered the lace design, which for the regiments in question were: 42nd, red stripe; 71st, red stripe; 72nd, green stripe.

No attempt is made in the chart to differentiate between the different tartans, but all seem to resemble the 'government' or 'Black Watch' sett: the 78th wore it with red and white overstripes, the 79th had Cameron of Erracht tartan, and the 92nd Gordon tartan. The 71st and 72nd are shown incorrectly as wearing kilts but in fact both ceased to wear Highland dress in 1809. Officers' lace for the 4th and 91st are shown as silver, whereas the former had changed to gold in 1809 and the latter probably about 1803.

Also shown here are the Ordnance services, the lighter blue of the Royal Engineers representing the 'Garter blue' facings worn by these officers. The Royal Artillery cadets are shown with a blue collar with a red patch; and the Royal Horse Artillery unaccountably with red lapels, which were not worn. Below these appear charts for the rifle-armed part of the 60th Foot and for the Royal Marines. On the charts of the eight West India Regiments (see Plate 46) the part-coloured panel represents the facing colour on the left and the red collar, and the shape at the right shows the half-lapel; facing-colours were yellow, save for the 1st white, 5th green and 8th grey.

In December 1802 it was ordered that the units of Invalids (soldiers unfit for front-line service) should be formed into seven Royal Garrison Battalions. In July 1804 these were re-named Royal Veteran Battalions, and a further five were raised between 1804 and 1808, and the 13th at Lisbon in March 1813. All were employed largely on garrison duty, and were disbanded between 1814 and 1818. The other units shown in this plate are covered in the Introduction (pp.24–25), except for the Garrison Battalions and Canadian units which are mentioned in the text to Plate 51.

REGULAR INFANTRY CONTINUED.

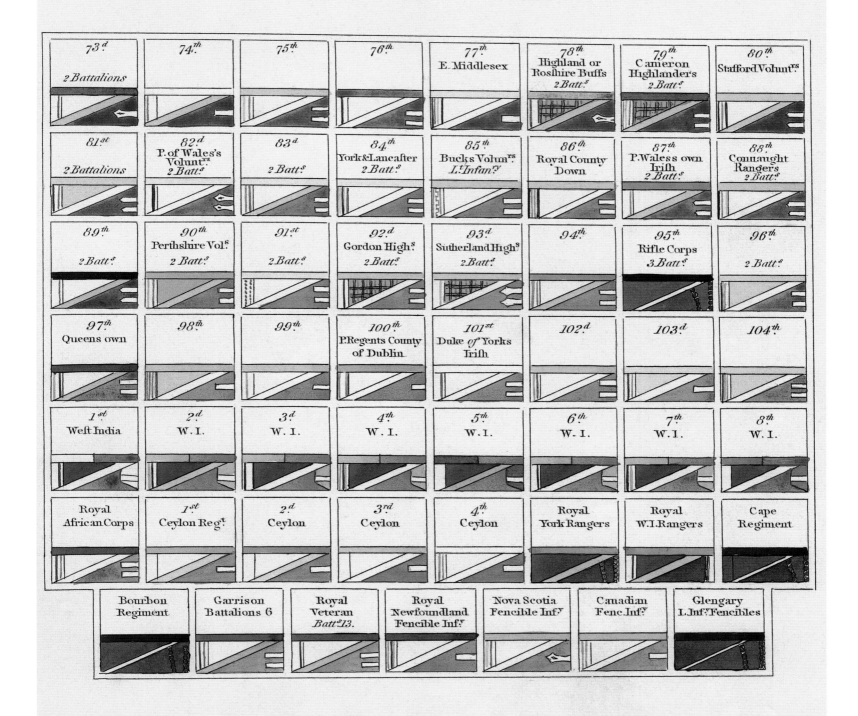

73.ᵈ 2 Battalions	74.ᵗʰ	75.ᵗʰ	76.ᵗʰ	77.ᵗʰ E. Middlesex	78.ᵗʰ Highland or Roshire Buffs 2 Batt.ˢ	79.ᵗʰ Cameron Highlanders 2 Batt.ˢ	80.ᵗʰ Stafford Volunt.ʳˢ
81.ˢᵗ 2 Battalions	82.ᵈ P. of Wales's Volunt.ʳˢ 2 Batt.ˢ	83.ᵈ 2 Batt.ˢ	84.ᵗʰ York & Lancaster 2 Batt.ˢ	85.ᵗʰ Bucks Volun.ʳˢ L.ᵗ Infan.ʸ	86.ᵗʰ Royal County Down	87.ᵗʰ P. Wales's own Irish 2 Batt.ˢ	88.ᵗʰ Connaught Rangers 2 Batt.ˢ
89.ᵗʰ 2 Batt.ˢ	90.ᵗʰ Perthshire Vol.ˢ 2 Batt.ˢ	91.ˢᵗ 2 Batt.ˢ	92.ᵈ Gordon High.ˢ 2 Batt.ˢ	93.ᵈ Sutherland High.ˢ 2 Batt.ˢ	94.ᵗʰ	95.ᵗʰ Rifle Corps 3 Batt.ˢ	96.ᵗʰ 2 Batt.ˢ
97.ᵗʰ Queens own	98.ᵗʰ	99.ᵗʰ	100.ᵗʰ P. Regents County of Dublin	101.ˢᵗ Duke of Yorks Irish	102.ᵈ	103.ᵈ	104.ᵗʰ
1.ˢᵗ West India	2.ᵈ W. I.	3.ᵈ W. I.	4.ᵗʰ W. I.	5.ᵗʰ W. I.	6.ᵗʰ W. I.	7.ᵗʰ W. I.	8.ᵗʰ W. I.
Royal African Corps	1.ˢᵗ Ceylon Reg.ᵗ	2.ᵈ Ceylon	3.ʳᵈ Ceylon	4.ᵗʰ Ceylon	Royal York Rangers	Royal W.I. Rangers	Cape Regiment

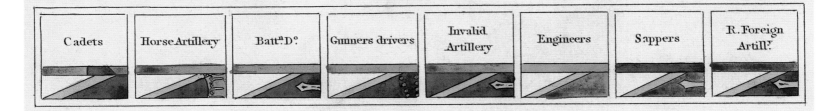

| Bourbon Regiment | Garrison Battalions 6 | Royal Veteran Batt.ⁿˢ 13. | Royal Newfoundland Fencible Inf.ʸ | Nova Scotia Fencible Inf.ʸ | Canadian Fenc. Inf.ʸ | Glengary L. Inf.ʸ Fencibles |

ROYAL ARTILLERY.

| Cadets | Horse Artillery | Batt.ⁿ D.º | Gunners drivers | Invalid Artillery | Engineers | Sappers | R. Foreign Artill.ʸ |

5.ᵗʰ & 7.ᵗʰ Battalions & Rifle Companies 60.ᵗʰ

Royal Marines 4 Divisions

Artillery, Engineers, Transport and Other Services

PLATE 39

Royal Artillery

(published February 1815)

As described in the Introduction (pp.20–21), the Royal Regiment of Artillery comprised both Foot and mounted ('Horse') branches; the style of their uniforms was based very closely upon the prevailing infantry and cavalry uniforms respectively, in the distinctive colouring of the Royal Artillery: dark blue with scarlet facings and yellow lace (gold lace for officers).

The men illustrated here are members of the Foot Artillery, evidently serving in garrison at home; as for the infantry, their breeches and gaiters would have been replaced by grey overalls and short gaiters for service overseas. The dark blue jacket, of infantry cut, had red facings and yellow lace, including 'bastion' shaped loops. Both red and white turnbacks are recorded, and although plain shoulder straps are shown here, edged with lace, some other sources indicate yellow worsted tufts like those worn by infantry battalion companies. The 1812 shako was worn with a white plume and yellow cords – unusually, the latter are shown here passing around the rear as well as the front of the cap – and a brass plate. This resembled the infantry's crowned, rococo shield in outline, but bore a distinctive design consisting of the reversed and interlaced 'GR' cypher within a strap inscribed 'Royal Regt. of Artillery', with a mortar at the base of the strap and a flaming grenade at either side of the mortar; the same design was worn in gilt by officers. Their uniforms also resembled those of infantry officers in cut, with scarlet facings and gold lace, their button-loops sometimes being shown as pointed-ended. They wore epaulettes like those of the infantry.

Artillerymen were armed with muskets and carried a similar knapsack and personal equipment as the infantry, but their cartridge boxes were in white leather rather than black, and bore a brass badge, sometimes shown mounted upon a red cloth patch cut to its shape: a crown over a horizontal C-scroll inscribed with the name of the regiment and apparently sometimes the battalion number. The white leather shoulder belt might include a powder flask attached by a red cord, and a fitting on the front to hold artillery tools, vent-prickers and a small hammer, although this equipment was probably carried only by selected gunners. Numerous illustrations show a short sabre carried by some gunners, on a shoulder belt or instead of a bayonet; apparently it had a brass hilt with single knucklebow, as shown here, and a straight, 25-inch, extremely broad and heavy blade.

The men illustrated are manning artillery in a garrison or fortress: the piece of ordnance shown is extremely heavy and has a stepped 'garrison carriage' with small 'truck' wheels, instead of the lighter barrel and 'field carriage' with larger wheels used by field artillery. By this date, field guns generally had screw elevators, whereas the gun shown was elevated or depressed by the older method of the insertion or withdrawal of a 'quoin' beneath the barrel – this is the triangular-sectioned block which can be seen supporting the 'sealed' or cascabel end of the gun barrel. The wooden carriage is painted in what was known in British service as the 'common colour', a grey or greenish-grey shade, with iron fittings painted black with a little red paint added. Gun barrels were manufactured in both iron and 'brass' (actually a bronze alloy).

C.H.S   Aquatinted by I.C.Stadler.

ROYAL ARTILLERY.

PLATE 40
Royal Horse Artillery
(published February 1815)

The origin of the Royal Horse Artillery is given in the Introduction (p. 21). A typical establishment was described by Captain Alexander Cavalié Mercer for his 'G' Troop at the commencement of the Waterloo campaign: five 9-pounder guns and one 5½-inch howitzer, with eight horses each; nine ammunition waggons, six horses each; forge, curricle-cart and baggage-waggon, four horses each; spare wheel cart, six horses; six mounted detachments, eight horses each; mounts for two staff sergeants, collar-makers and farrier, five horses; 17 officers' horses, 30 spare horses and six baggage mules: a total of 220 horses and six mules for a complement of five officers, a surgeon, two staff-sergeants, three sergeants, three corporals, six bombardiers, two trumpeters, six craftsmen, 80 gunners and 84 drivers. The troop was divided into six 'subdivisions' (each comprising one gun, its crew, and one ammunition waggon) or three 'divisions' (each of two subdivisions plus an extra ammunition waggon), each division commanded by a lieutenant, each right subdivision by a sergeant, and each left subdivision by a corporal. Mercer commented that:

> 'Perhaps at this time a troop of horse-artillery was the completest thing in the army; and whether broken up into half-brigades under the first and second captains, or into divisions under their lieutenants, or subdivisions under their sergeants and corporals, still each body was a perfect whole.'[1]

The uniform of the Royal Horse Artillery was substantially unchanged from about 1799, and resembled the pre-1812 light dragoon uniform: a tail-less, braided jacket in artillery colouring (dark blue with red collar and cuffs, yellow braid), and either white breeches worn with high boots, or for service dress grey overalls with a red stripe on the outer seam. The head-dress was a 'Tarleton' light dragoon helmet with brass fittings, black turban and white plume, as shown here. Officers wore sashes; Mercer stated that they were crimson silk until 1815, when hussar-style barrelled sashes came into use, but it is likely that the latter were used earlier. Further items which enhanced the hussar-like appearance of the officers were sabretaches and pelisses.

Initially the gunners wore shoulder belts, replaced by waist belts, from which their sabre was suspended (their weapon was the 1796 light cavalry sabre). However, both types of belt were in use with different troops at the same time, for in December 1815 Mercer records how his new troop gave up their white cross belts to his old 'G' Troop, in exchange for the latter's waist belts, not a popular measure as it exhibited 'our old worn jackets in all their nakedness… our overalls were in rags… '.[2] The men were also armed with pistols, carried in their saddle holsters.

1. Mercer, Gen. A.C., *Journal of the Waterloo Campaign*, Edinburgh & London 1870, Vol. I, pp. 161–62; reprinted Da Capo Press, New York 1995.
2. *Ibid.*, Vol. II, p. 321.

ROYAL HORSE ARTILLERY.

Aquatinted by I.C.Stadler.

PLATE 41

Royal Artillery: Mounted Rockett [sic] Corps

(published January 1815)

Named after its inventor, Sir William Congreve Bt. (1772–1828), the Congreve rocket was one of the more unusual weapons used during the period – other classes of weapon were generally similar in all European armies but the rocket was used almost exclusively by the British Army and Navy. It was an explosive projectile of various sizes affixed to a stick, up to 24 feet in length, which was launched at the enemy in the way of a firework sky-rocket, either from a rocket-cart or, more usually, from an iron tripod launcher. The heavy rockets used for bombardment could have considerable effect – some 40,000 were fired at Copenhagen in 1807, for example – but Wellington was among those who questioned the morality of their use: he stated that he only accepted a rocket troop in the Peninsula in order to acquire their horses, as he had no wish to burn down any town and knew of no other use for rockets!

Nevertheless, although rockets were desperately inaccurate, on the battlefield they could have a devastating effect on morale. George Gleig of the 85th wrote that the confusion they caused:

'beggars all description... you see it coming yet know not how to avoid it. It skips and starts about from place to place in so strange a manner, that the chances are, when you are running to the right or left to get out of the way, that you run directly against it; and hence the absolute rout which a fire of ten or twelve rockets can create, provided they take effect. But it is a very uncertain weapon. It may indeed spread havoc among the enemy, but it may also turn back upon the people who use it.'[1]

In June 1813 a specific 'Rocket Brigade' was formed, expanded to two troops that December. One troop, under Captain Richard Bogue, went to northern Europe and served at Leipzig (where Bogue was killed) as the only British contingent present; the other served in the Peninsula and under Edward Whinyates at Waterloo, though for the latter campaign Wellington insisted that the troop be equipped with 6-pounder guns as well.

The 'Mounted Rocket Corps' adopted the uniform of the Royal Horse Artillery, with some distinctions, as Whinyates recalled:

'Their appointments (both of horse and man), however, differed from those of the Horse Artillery. They had a pouch belt, which the Horse Artillery did not. Each mounted man carried a fasces of three or four rocket sticks in a bucket in a manner similar to the mode lances and Dragoon carbines are carried. These sticks were carried on the right side of the horse. Besides these the centre of Threes carried a small trough on his saddle bag, in which the rockets were laid when fired, and every man in the Rocket Sections carried rockets in his holsters... the small flag attached to the rocket stick... was added by the Captain as an ornament, and was discontinued, and not part of the real equipment. The Horse appointments were those of the Light Cavalry, and the N.C. Officers and gunners had blue shabraques laced with yellow.'[2]

The shabraque shown bears in a corner a crown over the letters 'GPR', which must signify 'George Prince Regent'; the same letters are shown on shabraques in Congreve's own *Details of the Rocket System* (1814), albeit below a Prince of Wales's crest. Upon the valise is 'RARC', evidently representing 'Royal Artillery Rocket Corps'. In the background may be seen rocket-launching frames and the streaks of rockets in the sky.

1. Gleig, G.R., *The Subaltern*, Edinburgh 1872, p. 291; reprinted Leo Cooper, London 2001.
2. Siborne, Maj. Gen. H.T. (ed.), *Waterloo Letters*, London 1891, pp. 207–08; reprinted Greenhill Books, London 1993.

C.H.S.

Aquatinted by I.C.Stadler.

ROYAL ARTILLERY

MOUNTED ROCKETT CORPS.

PLATE 42
Royal Artillery Drivers
(published June 1815)

Transportation of the artillery and its vehicles was the responsibility of the Royal Artillery's Corps of Drivers. Originally the army's transport was dependent almost entirely upon teams and drivers hired from civilian contractors, who remained outside the army, a system in every way thoroughly unsatisfactory. In 1794 a Corps of Drivers was founded as part of the Royal Artillery, one of the most important acts of Charles, 3rd Duke of Richmond while Master-General of the Ordnance; but although the concept was vital, the resulting formation was evidently far from perfect.

By 1808 there were eight troops of 554 men each, each comprising five sections of 90 drivers, plus assorted craftsmen, 945 draught and 75 riding horses, commanded by a captain; ultimately there were eleven troops. The men were divided among the various artillery companies and troops, so that little supervision by their own officers was possible, leading to poor discipline and morale. Alexander Dickson, Wellington's best artillery commander in the Peninsula, reported on the sad state of the Corps of Drivers which he described an an 'Augean stable'; many officers, he claimed, were indifferent to their duty, escaped service by spurious claims of infirmity, and made no attempt to pay their men, whose money was in some cases years in arrears. One officer of the Royal Horse Artillery, William Swabey, writing in 1813 about a corporal of the Corps of Drivers who had been court-martialled for selling ammunition to a Portuguese (who would then probably re-sell it back to the army), referred to the Corps of Drivers as 'that nest of infamy',[1] which seems a not unreasonable description. The problems could have been solved by integrating the drivers completely with the gunners, but that did not occur until 1822.

For this period, two patterns of jacket are recorded. One resembled that of the Foot Artillery (Plate 39) but the other was as shown here, in the same colouring but with pointed cuffs, three rows of buttons on the breast, and a 'frame' of lace around the buttons. It is unclear exactly when these uniforms were used; sometimes it is stated that the Foot Artillery type was worn prior to that shown here, but it is possible that different companies wore different uniform, with the Foot Artillery jacket worn by drivers attached to that branch of the Corps. The Tarleton helmet was worn with both, with a blue turban; the grey overalls are shown with either one or two red stripes. The corps was armed with the 1796 light cavalry sabre.

This illustration also shows a baggage waggon, and the undress uniform, consisting of an undress jacket resembling a sleeved waistcoat, and a flat forage cap of the so-called 'Scotch bonnet' variety. The principal figure (right) is a corporal, his rank identified by the chevrons on the upper arm, and he is mounted on one of his company's 'riding horses'. The horse furniture is typical of that used generally on campaign, with pistol holsters at the front of the saddle and no shabraque.

1. Swabey, W., *Diary of Campaigns in the Peninsula*, London 1984, p. 176.

ROYAL ARTILLERY DRIVERS.

PLATE 43

A Field Officer of the Royal Engineers, and a Private Sapper
(published January 1815)

The organisation of the engineer services is described in the Introduction (pp. 21–22). The traditional uniform of the Royal Engineers had included a blue coat with black velvet facings and gold lace; this had one major disadvantage: as one engineer wrote, 'From our uniform being like that of the French we were sometimes mistaken for officers of that nation.'[1] Consequently, a new uniform was introduced in 1812, of scarlet with Garter-blue facings (a slightly lighter shade than the usual dark blue of ordinary 'royal' regiments), and gold lace.

Despite the disadvantage of the old uniform, the new one was not universally popular. One of the Peninsular army's most distinguished engineers, Major William Nicholas, wrote in April 1812, shortly before his death at Badajoz, that:

> 'Our uniform is changed to scarlet with a gold-laced dress-coat. I dislike the change on account of the colour and the expence [sic]; but I shall order nothing till I know whether I am to have the brevet rank; as it makes a difference in the epaulettes.'[2]

Some officers must have retained the blue uniform until near the end of the Peninsular War, for one engineer, Harry Jones, attributed to it his preservation from death while lying injured after the unsuccessful attack on San Sebastian in July 1813. As the French came out from their defences to stab the British wounded, a sergeant cried out, 'Oh mon Colonel, êtes-vous blessé?'; Jones recalled that:

> 'He must have mistaken my rank, from seeing a large gold bullion epaulette on my right shoulder, and the blue uniform, rendering it more conspicuous, and immediately ordered some of his men to remove me into the town.'[3]

The officer shown here wears the new uniform, with the two epaulettes of field rank; the long skirted pattern of coat and bicorn were retained, the engineers not adopting short jackets and shakos as did infantry officers.

Similarly, the Royal Military Artificers wore blue jackets with black facings, but the new Royal Sappers and Miners changed their jacket-colour like the engineers; they wore infantry-style uniform in red, with blue facings and yellow 'bastion' loops, with the 1812 shako with white plume, white breeches and black gaiters for dress and grey overalls for service. The man shown by Hamilton Smith is armed with a short sabre, probably like that of the artillery, upon a shoulder belt, and is carrying pegs and line to lay out the position of trenches or a besieging-battery, as indicated by the officer, preparatory to attacking the fortress whose guns are firing in the background. In working dress, the sappers wore short-skirted, single breasted red jackets with blue collar and cuffs, no lace, and dark grey-blue overalls with a red stripe, and small, peak-less leather undress caps bearing the initials 'RS&M' in brass on the front. The companies at Cadiz are recorded as having overalls with a black stripe, and grey cloth forage caps with black braid and bearing the initials on the left side.

1. Jones, R., *An Engineer Officer under Wellington in the Peninsula*, ed. Capt. H.V. Shore, Cambridge 1986, p. 11.
2. *Royal Military Chronicle*, February 1813, p. 271.
3. Jones, H., 'Narrative of Seven Weeks' Captivity in St. Sebastian', in *United Service Journal* 1841, Vol. I, p. 193.

A FIELD OFFICER of ROYAL ENGINEERS,

and A PRIVATE SAPPER.

PLATE 44

Cavalry Staff Corps 1813

(published May 1813)

Campaigning in the Peninsular War demonstrated a need for a provost or police unit to help combat crime and desertion. There was also a shortage of reliable orderlies, who were normally taken from cavalry regiments, and not always with success: a well-known incident concerned an order from Sir David Baird which went astray during the retreat to Corunna: 'By God, the rascal of a dragoon by whom I sent those despatches this morning, has got drunk and lost them'![1] Accordingly, in April 1813, four troops of 'Staff Corps of Cavalry' were created, two at home and two (of 11 officers and 132 other ranks each) in the Peninsula. For this earliest attempt to form a permanent corps of military police, the men selected for it were those of the highest probity and reliability. The corps was disbanded on 25 September 1814, but was re-formed in 1815 (when it was intended to rank in seniority after the cavalry and before the Foot Guards), and lasted until December 1818.

The uniform selected appears to have been intended as a cavalry version of that of the existing Royal Staff Corps (see Plate 4), with the Tarleton helmet, but more appropriately it was the new light dragoon style that was actually adopted, in red with blue facings and white piping, girdles of red and blue, overalls with double blue stripes and the new light dragoon shako with white lace, white metal chin-scales and, uniquely, a red plume. Officers' lace was silver and their rank distinctions like those of the light dragoons. The horse furniture depicted includes a dark blue saddle cloth edged red – its size hardly qualifies it as a shabraque – and a cylindrical red valise inscribed 'SD/A', the significance of which is explained by Hamilton Smith's chart (Plate 51) where the unit appears as 'Staff Dragoons' to which the 'A' would appear to have been added as a troop identification letter. The figure in the background, who carries a carbine suspended from his shoulder belt, may have alternative horse furniture of a white sheepskin saddle cover, but this is not clear.

1. Napier, W.F.P., *History of the War in the Peninsula, and in the South of France*, London 1832, Vol. I, p. xxviii.

CAVALRY STAFF CORPS 1813

PLATE 45

An Officer [L], Private [R] & Driver of the Royal Waggon Train

(published April 1812)

The weaknesses of the army's transport organisation are mentioned in the Introduction (p. 22), and were not solved by the creation in 1799 of the Royal Waggon Train, even though it was an improvement on the previous Corps of Royal Waggoners. The comparatively small size of the new unit could only solve a fraction of the army's transport problems, and apparently it did not receive universal praise. For example, writing in 1808, Commissary Augustus Schaumann described how the unit's commander, 'Fat General [Digby] Hamilton of the wagon train has also turned up here with his useless wagon corps.'[1]

Not all the unit's members were deserving of such condemnation; it is possible that the bravery of one man saved Hougoumont at the Battle of Waterloo. The defenders of this fortified post were running out of cartridges and an ADC went in search of a re-supply. He encountered a private of the Royal Waggon Train with a tumbril of ammunition and explained the problem, but was unwilling to order the man to act because of the hazardous nature of the task. The man never hesitated, however, but drove the cart through heavy fire and into the beleaguered post, and it was said that the successful defence of this vital position was only possible because of his great heroism. His identity was not recorded at the time, but he was probably Joseph Brewer, who later transferred to the 3rd Foot Guards (one of the units he had re-supplied), and that regiment awarded him a medal.

Originally the Royal Waggon Train wore blue uniforms – hence its nickname 'Newgate Blues' (derived from Newgate prison), which is perhaps some indication of how it was regarded. In 1811, however, it changed to the red uniform illustrated here. For the rank and file, it included a jacket with dark blue facings (including pointed cuffs), white lace, and three rows of buttons on the breast, surrounded by a 'frame' of lace like that worn by the Artillery drivers. Hamilton Smith shows the driver in blue breeches and riding boots, the dismounted man in grey pantaloons or overalls, with short black gaiters; the head-dress is a cylindrical shako with white cords and white over red plume. Officers wore markedly different uniform, the rear of which is shown precisely by Hamilton Smith, when compared with an existing garment: a short-tailed jacket with blue collar and 'indented' cuffs, the breast covered with silver braid and three rows of silver buttons in hussar style, with six Vs of lace on the cuff and skirt, and two lace loops at each side of the collar. Hamilton Smith shows the officer wearing a bicorn hat, but there is also evidence of the use of the 1812 light dragoon shako with a silver lace band and rosette and silver chin-scales. The officer is shown here with a 1796 light cavalry sabre suspended from a waist belt, possibly of black leather to match the black shoulder belts worn by the private.

1. Schaumann, A.L.F., *On the Road with Wellington*, ed. A.M. Ludovici, London 1924, p. 87; reprinted with Introduction by B. Cornwell, Greenhill Books, London 1999.

An OFFICER, PRIVATE & DRIVER of the
ROYAL WAGGON TRAIN.

Foreign Regiments
and the
Militia of Great Britain and Ireland

PLATE 46

A Private of the 5th West India Regiment
(published January 1815)

Some details of the history and composition of the West India Regiments is given in the Introduction (pp. 22–23). The 5th Regiment, illustrated in this plate, was raised as Howe's Regiment in 1795 and numbered as the 5th West India Regiment in 1798. Between that date and the abolition of the slave trade in 1807, more than 87 per cent of its recruits were Africans (the policy of recruiting Africans, instead of those already resident in the West Indies, was one which received some criticism). The 1st and 5th West India Regiments formed part of the expedition against New Orleans in the winter of 1814–15; unprepared for the cold and wet climate, both regiments suffered terribly from the conditions. Alexander Dickson of the artillery described how they were prostrated by the cold, while another officer stated that 'many of the poor blacks being frost-bitten, [they were] quite incapable of doing duty'.[1]

Although the uniform and equipment of the West India Regiments were based upon that of the British infantry, there were significant differences. The 1802 regulations described the jacket as short-tailed, without turnbacks but 'cut to slope off behind', with half-lapels, pointed cuffs and shoulder straps in the facing colour but with a red collar, the collar and cuffs laced round, with three loops on each lapel and one on the collar. About 1810–12 the original, square-cut half-lapels changed to the 'shield' shape illustrated (with a pointed lower edge); the cuffs changed to the ordinary infantry pattern, with lace loops, and Hamilton Smith's plate omits the collar lace (although the lace edging appears to have been drawn in but not coloured). The three sets of loops on the lapels are still present, but now conform in length to the re-shaping of the lapels.

Originally the West India Regiments were issued with white, one-piece gaiter-trousers, but from July 1810 these were changed to blue serge. Until 1803 they wore 'round hats', and shakos thereafter, with the 1812 pattern evidently being issued in due course. Originally they wore black leather equipment, which probably remained in use for some time after the official specification of white belts in October 1802. Hamilton Smith shows the regimental belt plate as bearing the number 'V'. Waistcoats were not issued, but for drill and undress there were tail-less white jackets, resembling a sleeved waistcoat, with collar and cuffs in the regimental facing colour; this was worn with white trousers, as shown in the background of this plate. The man shown in undress has bare feet; most of the recruits would have been unused to wearing shoes or boots.

Another man in the background wears white overalls and short gaiters, in the style of the British infantry. Like all the surviving West India Regiments, except for the 1st and 2nd which remained in existence, the 5th was disbanded in 1817–18.

1. 'Old Sub', in *United Service Journal* 1840, Vol. II, p. 195.

A PRIVATE of the 5ᵗʰ WEST INDIA REGIMENT.

PLATE 47
3rd Hussars [R], Infantry [L] & L[ight] Infantry, King's German Legion
(published April 1815)

The history and composition of the King's German Legion are covered in the Introduction (pp. 23–24). Their uniforms were styled upon the respective branches of the British Army, as evident from this plate.

The infantry had blue facings, their lace with a blue line and with loops in pairs, with gold lace for officers. Hamilton Smith shows a grenadier of a line battalion (left), identified by his white plume; the Legion is shown with blue shoulder wings instead of the red normally worn by British flank companies. This shows a further example of the shako cords suspended around the rear of the cap, instead of just at the front which appears to have been more common. The Legion's shako plate resembled that of the ordinary infantry, a crowned rococo shield bearing the raised cypher 'GR' over a horizontal-oval strap bearing the name of the Legion, surrounding a numeral which identified the individual battalion. The belt plate was of an oval shape in brass (gilt for officers), bearing an upright-oval strap carrying the title of the unit, with a lion atop the strap and a crown inside it. The line battalions maintained companies of sharpshooters armed with Baker rifles, who wore the green plume of light companies and carried belts of 'rifle' style, like those of the ordinary rifle corps but in white leather instead of black.

The Legion's two Light Battalions wore dark green 'rifle-style' uniform, but with certain differences. The 1st Light Battalion had single breasted jackets with black-edged wings, and wore a shako with an upright plume; the 2nd Light Battalion had jackets of rifle-corps style, with three rows of buttons on the breast and shoulder straps ending in black tufts, and shakos with cords and a ball-shaped pompom. Both had black facings. The charts (Plate 51) indicate the jacket with three rows of buttons and white piping for both battalions (as shown here), and this plate also shows a form of 'mirliton' hussar cap instead of a more conventional, peaked shako, with the cords seemingly more appropriate to those of the 2nd Light Battalion. (Some rifle corps, including the 95th, had caps with a peak which could be folded back to resemble a mirliton cap more closely than a shako, though this appears to have been predominantly an officers' style.)

Initially, only a proportion of the men of the light battalions were armed with rifles, the remainder carrying muskets, but it was noted in the Peninsula that the rifles of casualties were usually distributed among the unwounded men, so that the proportion of rifles to muskets increased. As late as 1814 only some 60 per cent of the light battalion men were armed with rifles, but in the Waterloo campaign it seems as if all were rifle-armed. It was largely the 2nd Light Battalion which carried out the heroic defence of La Haye Sainte, until the survivors were forced out of the place after they had run out of ammunition, their rifles not being able to use the ordinary musket ammunition which was presumably was all that was available for immediate re-supply.

The uniform of the Legion's cavalry is described in the Introduction (p. 24), the 1st–3rd Hussars wearing hussar dress even before they were officially titled as such. They wore fur caps, but Hamilton Smith shows a light dragoon shako.

It is possible that Hamilton Smith chose to illustrate the 3rd Hussars as a result of personal observation. Raised in 1806 and clothed as hussars from the beginning, having served in the Corunna campaign, the regiment was at home from July 1809. Hamilton Smith could therefore have seen them in Britain. The 3rd next went abroad in 1813, landing in North Germany in August of that year, for the campaign in which they won the battle-honour of Göhrde.

3RD HUSSARS, INFANTRY & L. INFANTRY.

KINGS GERMAN LEGION.

PLATE 48

York Light Infantry Volunteers:
A Serjeant in Morning Parade Dress, A Private on Duty
(published December 1813)

The York Light Infantry Volunteers originated in September 1803 when the Dutch troops which had been in garrison in the South American colonies of Berbice, Demerara and Essequibo volunteered to enter British service, after those places had been occupied by the British.

The garrison of Berbice had mutinied in the previous May, against the then government of Holland, the French satellite Batavian Republic, and in favour of Britain. Most of these troops, principally from Berbice, were formed into a British 'foreign corps' at Barbados, initially titled as the Barbados Volunteer Emigrants; in 1804 the title was changed to the York Light Infantry Volunteers, in honour of the Duke of York. In April 1804 the unit took part in the capture of Surinam, in 1809 in the capture of Martinique and in 1810 in the capture of Guadeloupe. Its strength increased progressively, from 650 men in ten companies in 1807, to 1,290 in twelve companies in October 1809 and to in excess of 1,500 by 1811. It served in various garrisons in the West Indies throughout its existence, was reduced to ten companies in December 1816, and in March 1817 was disbanded at Harwich.

Despite the foreign nature of its personnel, many of the officers were British; in August 1814, for example, 36 officers appear to have been British, and only 23 foreign. Such corps were generally not popular with those British officers who were in a position to choose their units, but many were commissioned NCOs who initially had little choice. Patrick Masterson of the 87th, for example, in reward for the capture of the Eagle at Barrosa (see Plate 35), was commissioned in the regiment, as was Sergeant William Newman of the 43rd Light Infantry, transferring from an ensigncy in the 1st West India Regiment, awarded for his courage on the retreat to Corunna.

As shown in this plate, the regiment wore a uniform based upon that of the 95th: dark green with black facings, white piping and three rows of buttons on the breast. The sergeant shown in 'morning parade dress' wears his undress, tail-less sleeved waistcoat in white with black collar, cuffs and shoulder straps, white undress trousers, a sash without the usual facing-coloured stripe, and carries what appears to be a blanket made up into a pack. Unlike the 95th, the regiment used white belts. The sergeant appears to carry a light fusil with the stock cut back from the muzzle, and has no bayonet but a sword that resembles a French *sabre briquet*, perhaps a weapon captured during the campaigning in the West Indies.

Originally the regiment would have worn the 'stovepipe' shako, but Hamilton Smith shows a rare depiction of the 1812 cap as produced for service in tropical climates. Here, and in other sources, such shakos are shown as white, although sample patterns supplied to the Prince of Wales are described as being made of drab-coloured felt with tan leatherwork, and an Inspection Return of the York Light Infantry Volunteers refers to brown shakos. The shako cords appear to be unplaited and hung all around the cap, and there is a marked difference in plumes, that of the private being a small worsted tuft, while the sergeant has a larger, feather plume.

YORK LIGHT INFANTRY VOLUNTEERS.

A SERJEANT in MORNING PARADE DRESS,

A PRIVATE on DUTY.

PLATE 49

Foreign Corps in the British Service:
Privates of the Greek Light Infantry Regiment
(published December 1813)

This exotically-dressed unit arose out of British operations in the Mediterranean, notably the occupation of the Ionian Islands of Zante, Cephalonia, Ithaca and Kithera in October 1807, territories deemed to belong to Napoleon according to the Treaty of Tilsit, but whose inhabitants favoured independence or at least administration by the British. Commander of the British expedition was Major-General Sir John Oswald, whose staff included Captain Richard Church of the Royal Corsican Rangers. His suggestion of raising a corps of Greeks for British service was approved, and in March 1810 he was given command of a unit styled Greek Light Infantry, raised in part from Suliote tribesmen from the mainland, with their own chiefs, or Albanians, as officers. In the same month they took part in the British attack on Santa Maura, with mixed success, they:

> 'no sooner came within the smell of powder than they assumed the attitude of adoration used by Mussulmans to the Prophet: they remained prone on their faces until the 35th [Foot] passed them. This attachment to the soil, although an amenable feeling in some instances, is rather inconvenient in the case of storming a fort. The title of this regiment was evidently a misnomer; no troops could better deserve the name of *heavy* infantry than those who became altogether immovable.'[1]

Nevertheless, Oswald was satisfied with their potential when their natural light infantry skills should be employed properly, and became their colonel when the unit was taken onto the British establishment as the Duke of York's Greek Light Infantry in March 1811. In 1812 Church returned to Britain to recover his health, and was commissioned to raise and command a second unit, of four companies, styled the Greek Light Infantry, the corps illustrated here.

Hamilton Smith's plate of this second unit – described on Plate 51 as the 2nd Battalion – shows a very similar uniform to that of the 1st or Duke of York's, which is shown by Goddard & Booth's *Military Costume of Europe*: a collar-less red jacket worn over a red waistcoat, with green cuffs and trimming for the 2nd and yellow for the 1st. Beneath these garments the traditional Greek *fustanella* (a long, white, kilt-like shirt) was worn over white knee-length trousers, with red stockings and short boots or sandals of local manufacture. Goddard and Booth show a red skull-cap, Hamilton Smith a cap with a facing-coloured tuft and evidently a brass badge bearing the royal cypher. The men shown are equipped as riflemen, with powder horns and black leather equipment, and a holstered pistol (these were issued to the first corps in November 1811). The brass-hilted short sword was actually a bayonet, for Goddard & Booth show it 'fixed' on the rifle. Officers' uniforms were rather more elaborate, Goddard & Booth showing a white pagri around the cap, and a crimson shoulder-sash, while Denis Dighton depicted a very ornate costume including a combed helmet with horsehair mane.[2]

The 1st or Duke of York's participated in the expedition to Genoa (April 1814) and was disbanded in January 1816; the 2nd Regiment was disbanded in October 1814. Subsequently Sir Richard Church (1784–1873) accepted command of the Greek forces in the War of Independence and became famous as 'the liberator of Greece'.

1. *United Service Journal* 1840, Vol. III, p. 331.
2. See Haswell Miller, A.E., & Dawnay, N.P., *Military Drawings and Paintings in the Royal Collection*, London 1966, Vol. I, fig. 305.

FOREIGN CORPS IN THE BRITISH SERVICE.

PRIVATES of the GREEK LIGHT INFANTRY REGIMENT.

C.H.S.

Aquatinted by I.C.Stadler.

PLATE 50
Hussars and Infantry of the Duke Of Brunswick Oels's Corps
(published July 1812)

As described in the Introduction (p. 24), Duke Friedrich Wilhelm of Brunswick formed his 'Legion' in 1809. To emphasize the nature of his cause, his troops were dressed in black and used as their insignia a skull and crossed bones, hence their unofficial name of 'Black Legion'. Following the corps' evacuation from Germany it entered British service, in two formations: a hussar regiment of six troops, four of which served in eastern Spain in 1813, Sicily in 1814, and at Genoa 1815–16; and a regiment of infantry. This was styled the Brunswick Oels Jägers, went to the Peninsula in 1810, served first with the Light Division and from about April 1811 with the 7th Division. Three of the twelve companies were detached to the 4th and 5th Divisions to supplement the skirmishing facility of those formations, in the same way that companies of the 5/60th were distributed throughout the army. The calibre of the original recruits could not be maintained and foreigners of various origins were drafted in, and desertion became a great problem. Jonathan Leach of the 95th recalled that, 'They deserted to the French in such numbers, that we had a lease of them but for a few weeks',[1] while Major-General Robert 'Black Bob' Craufurd (1764–1812) of the Light Division is said to have remarked that if any of the Brunswickers 'have a wish to go over to the enemy, let them express it, and I give them my word of honour I will grant them a pass to that effect instantly, for we are better without such.'[2] The infantry returned home and left British service on 25 December 1814, although the hussars remained in British service until 25 July 1816.

The Brunswick contingent which participated in the Waterloo campaign as part of Wellington's army was largely newly raised and not formally in British service, although the men continued to wear mainly black uniforms similar to the ones illustrated and described here.

In British service the Brunswick Oels Jägers and Hussars retained the black uniforms with light blue facings that they had worn originally, with the addition of British rank markings (the chevrons worn by the two sergeants shown here, and the crimson waist-sash with light blue stripe worn by the infantry sergeant). The Jägers in the Peninsula appear to have worn the short, braided jacket shown for the figure at the right, although Hamilton Smith also depicts the infantry sergeant in the old, thigh-length *litewka* (frock-coat) worn in 1809, and evidently still in use when he executed his drawings. The skull and crossed bones carried on the shako and upon the hussar's shabraque shown here led to their nickname in British service of 'Death or Glory men'. In the Peninsula their sharpshooter companies – presumably those detached from the main body – wore green jackets with light blue facings and grey overalls, and carried rifles; the remainder were armed with muskets.

1. Leach, J., *Rough Sketches of the Life of an Old Soldier*, London 1831, p. 191; reprinted Trotman, London 1999.
2. Costello, E., *Adventures of a Soldier, written by Himself*, London 1852; 1967 edn., ed. A. Brett-James, p. 47.

HUSSARS and INFANTRY of the DUKE of BRUNSWICK OELS'S CORPS.

Aquatinted by I.C.Stadler.

PLATE 51

Foreign Corps 1813 & 1814, King's German Legion &c.

The charts which comprise Plates 38 and 51 include a number of 'Foreign Corps', details of most of which are covered in the Introduction (pp. 24–26).

Following the re-naming of the Royal Garrison Battalions as Royal Veteran Battalions in 1804, in February 1805 three new Garrison Battalions were created from the sixteen 'Battalions of Reserve' formed under the Additional Forces Act of July 1803. In 1806 the number of Garrison Battalions was increased to nine, but in the chart on Plate 38 only six are indicated, the 9th having become the 103rd Foot in 1808, and the 7th and 8th having been disbanded in March 1810. Plate 51 illustrates further Garrison units. Two European Garrison Companies were formed in the West Indies in December 1805, from members of British regiments in the region no longer fit for full active service; the 1st was formed in Jamaica and the 2nd in Barbados. From 1808 to April 1814 both were stationed in the Bahamas, before returning to Jamaica; the 2nd was disbanded in April 1814 and the 1st in June 1817. The Black Garrison Company was formed in Jamaica in August 1813 from men of the 2nd, 5th and 7th West India Regiments who were unfit for active service; a 2nd Company was formed in June 1815, and both were disbanded in July 1817. Details of the New South Wales Company are given in the Introduction (p. 26).

Four Canadian corps are shown in Plate 38, and a fifth in Plate 51. The Royal Newfoundland Fencibles were authorised in June 1803, served in the War of 1812 and were disbanded in June 1816; contrary to the chart, their officers appear to have had gold lace. The Nova Scotia Fencibles were authorised in July 1803, and disbanded in July 1816. The Canadian Fencibles were authorised in August 1803 and disbanded in June 1816; contrary to the chart, a tailor's specifications suggest that the lace loops were borne in pairs.

Formed largely from Scottish settlers in Canada, the Glengarry Light Infantry was authorised in February 1812 and saw much distinguished service in the War of 1812; although armed with smoothbore muskets, it was dressed as a rifle corps. (The spelling 'Glengary' on the chart is incorrect.) The green uniform was found to be of great value when skirmishing: it was recorded that they:

> 'always skirmish in a partly cleared country, better than our red jackets. The Yankies [sic] used to call them "Tarnation black stumps", as they could stand in a field with the stumps, and at some distance scarcely be distinguished from them, owing to the colour of their uniform.'[1]

The New Brunswick Fencibles (Plate 51) were formed in October 1812 and disbanded in February 1816. Initially they were supposed to wear the uniform of the previous New Brunswick Fencibles (taken into the line as the 104th Foot in 1810), but the chart shows light yellow instead of pale buff facings; but in reality these may never have been worn, as the unit was clothed in uniforms intended for the New Brunswick Militia, probably with white facings.

Shown in Plate 51 are charts of staff appointments and miscellaneous other units, details of which are included in the text to the plates which illustrate their respective uniforms; the parti-coloured horizontal bands in the charts represent collars with facing-coloured patches. Also illustrated are the army's 'civil' departments, those of the Commissary-General, Paymaster-General and Storekeeper-General, whose staff wore a uniform similar to the army staff but in dark blue with black facings.

1. *United Service Journal* 1841, Vol. I, p. 558.

FOREIGN CORPS 1813 & 1814.

KING'S GERMAN LEGION &c.

CAVALRY.

INFANTRY.

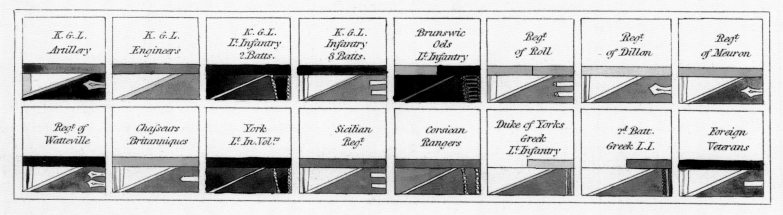

ADDITIONAL BATTALIONS 1814.

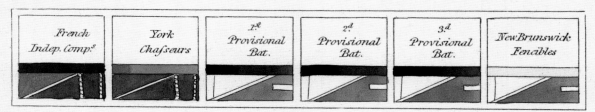

STAFF OF THE ARMY.

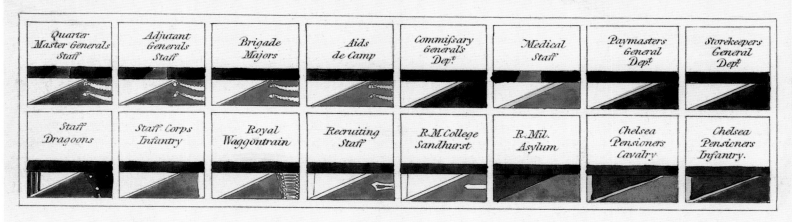

GARRISON COMPANIES.

PLATE 52
Facings of the Militia of Great Britain and Ireland, 1814

This plate illustrates the uniform of the county militias, arranged in order of their precedence numbers, as described in the Introduction (pp. 26–27). Unlike the Scottish regiments, which from 1803 were integrated in the same precedence list as the English and Welsh, the Irish regiments maintained their own precedence numbers throughout. These were established by a ballot drawn in August 1793, which remained unchanged throughout the period, with two exceptions. In the original ballot, rank no. 9 was occupied by the Down Militia, and no. 24 by the Drogheda battalion. In May 1797 the latter was incorporated in the Louth Militia, leaving rank no. 24 vacant; it was filled when the large Down regiment was divided into two in April 1800, so that from that date rank no. 9 was occupied by the Royal South Down, and no. 24 by the Royal North Down.

The county militias wore uniforms of the prevailing line infantry style, with regimental distinctions in the form of facing colour, lace and insignia. Hamilton Smith's chart is an important source for the details of other ranks' lace, though as for the regular regiments, alternative colourings do exist (for example, two red stripes for Berwick, one red and one yellow for Forfar, two blue stripes for North Lincoln, one red and one black for North Hants, one yellow for the Isle of Wight, one red and one yellow stripe for Renfrew). The lace designs for two regiments in this copy appear not to have been filled in: other copies show Ross with a green stripe and the Royal Middlesex (Westminster) with the same blue stripe as the other two Middlesex corps.

Four of the Welsh militia regiments were uniformed as rifle corps, the Royal Pembroke from 1811, the Royal Carnarvon[1] and Royal Flint in 1812, and the Royal Denbigh in 1813, the last retaining its dark blue facings with the new green uniform. In addition, although not shown, the North York Militia maintained a detachment of green-clad 'light armed marksmen', equipped as riflemen. Of the facing colours, that of the East and West Kent is deserving of mention, being a light blue-grey known as 'Kentish grey', a shade not worn by any regular regiment. In some cases it is difficult to identify black facings from blue in the chart: black was worn by the regiments numbered 9, 15 (North), 16, 19, 44, 46, 54, 64 and 71, and in the Irish list 4, 18, 31 and 36; the rest blue. Buff facings may be distinguished from various shades of yellow in those cases where the colour of facings and breeches are the same, regiments with buff facings having buff breeches as well.

Shown in Plate 51 are three 'Provisional Battalions'; these were also formed from militiamen, who had volunteered to serve in the Peninsular War, where they arrived just too late to participate in any action; further details are given in the Introduction (p. 27).

---

1. 'Carnarvon' was the preferred contemporary spelling, used in the *Army List* and Hamilton Smith's chart, rather than the more modern Caernarvon or Caernarfon.

FACINGS of the MILITIA
OF
GREAT BRITAIN & IRELAND,
1814.

MILITIA of GREAT BRITAIN.

1 Berwick	2 Stafford	3 Shropshire	4 R.Denbeigh L.I.	5 Ross	6 R.Cheshire	7 R.S.Glocester	7 R.N.Glocester	8 Wiltshier	9 1st Sumerset
9 2nd Somerset	10 Inverness	11 Forfar	12 Oxford	13 Bedford	14 N.Lincoln	14 S.Lincoln	15 North Hants	15 South Hants	15 Isle of Wight
16 R.Carnarvon L.I.	17 R.Westmort	18 R Monmouth & Brecon	19 R.Flint L.I.	20 R.Middlesex East	20 R.Middlesex West	20 R.Middlesex Westminster	21 Kirkudbright	22 Renfrew	23 R.Radnor L.I.
24 Cambridge	25 Durham	26 R.Montgomery L.I.	27 R.Cardigan L.I.	28 Stirling	29 Northampton	30 E.Essex	30 W.Essex	31 R.Cornwall L.I.	32 West York 1
32 West York 2	32 West York 3	33 Hertford	34 Fife	35 R.Cornwall & Devon Miners L.I.	36 Leicester	37 R.Berks	38 Ayr	39 R.Caermarthen Fusiliers	40 Warwick
41 R.Surrey	41 R.Surrey	42 R.Glamorgan	43 Argyll	44 N.York	45 R.Lanark	46 E.Norfolk	46 W.Norfolk	47 Worcester	48 Sussex
49 R.Bucks	50 Dorset	51 Edinburgh	52 1 R.Lancashire	52 2 R.Lancashire	52 3 R.Lancashire	53 R.Cumberland	54 R.Pembroke Rifle	55 Aberdeen	56 R Tower Hamlets 1
56 R.Tower Hamlets 2	57 East Kent	57 West Kent	58 R.London East	58 R.London West	59 E.Suffolk	59 W.Suffolk	60 Northumberland	61 Hereford	62 Derby
63 Rutland L.I.	64 Huntingdon	65 R.Merioneth	66 East Devon	66 North Devon	66 South Devon	67 York E.Riding	68 R.Perth	69 R.Anglesea L.I.	70 Dumfries

71 Nottingham	## MILITIA of IRELAND.							1 Monaghan	2 Tyrone
3 Mayo North	4 Kildare	5 Louth	6 Westmeath	7 Antrim	8 Armagh	9 R.S.Down	10 Leitrim	11 Galway	12 City Dublin
13 Limerick City	14 Kerry	15 Longford	16 Londonderry	17 Meath	18 Cavan	19 Kings County	20 Kilkenny	21 Co.Limerick	22 Sligo
23 Carlow	24 R.N.Down	25 Queens County	26 Clare	27 City Cork	28 Tipperary	29 Fermanagh	30 South Mayo	31 Roscommon	32 South Cork
33 Waterford	34 North Cork	35 Co:Dublin	36 Dunnegal	37 Wicklow	38 Wexford				

Reference.

a. Cuff and Collar
b. Coat & Shape of Privates Lace
c. Worm in the Lace
d. Breeches
e. Officers Lace

Royal Marines, Cadets
and Other British Subjects

PLATE 53
A Private of the Royal Marines
(published January 1815)

The history and organisation of the Corps of Royal Marines is given in the Introduction (pp. 27–28). By virtue of its date of formation, although the Corps was connected to the Admiralty, it was reckoned as ranking in terms of seniority between the 49th and 50th Regiments of Foot, but was not placed in that position in the *Army List*.

Dressed and equipped largely as infantry, the Marines initially wore white facings and a bicorn hat. The granting of the title 'Royal' necessitated a change of facing colour to blue, and officers' lace from silver to gold; the other ranks' lace apparently remained unchanged, white with red and blue lines, the loops square-ended and in pairs. Although officers continued to use the bicorn hat, for other ranks it was replaced in 1799 by the 'round hat' illustrated, with a white band and white-over-red plume (white for grenadiers and green for light companies, until these flank companies were discontinued in November 1804). White brim-edging was specified for the 'battalion' companies, but is not shown here. Officers' long-tailed coats were presumably replaced by the short-tailed infantry jacket in 1812.

The legwear shown was probably reserved for 'dress' occasions, with trousers worn on service, contemporary illustrations showing white or blue, or white gaiter-trousers. An order of December 1808 specified that the trousers should be dyed blue instead of grey, which was presumably the colour used before that date, and in December 1815 grey was specified in place of blue.

Equipment was of infantry style, the cartridge box bearing an eight-pointed brass star, with 'GR' in the centre within a circlet inscribed with the Corps' motto *Per Mare Per Terram* ('By Sea, By Land'). Although it is known that from about 1802 the belt plates were oblong, brass, bearing a crowned fouled anchor above a scroll inscribed 'Royal Marines' and with a laurel-spray below, there is evidence for other designs, including the oval version shown here. Hanging from the shoulder belt may be seen the wire 'picker' and brush, used to clean the lock of the musket.

In September 1810, in addition to those serving aboard ship, a 1st Marine Battalion was formed for service in the Peninsula; it served in garrison at Lisbon and subsequently executed a number of landings on the north coast of Spain, including that at Santander (which became the army's forward supply base); and a 2nd Battalion was sent to Santander in August 1812. Both battalions, and a 3rd formed in February 1813, served in North America during the War of 1812.

In addition to the ordinary marines, a company of Royal Marine Artillery was formed for each Division in 1804, to man the mortars and howitzers with which bomb-vessels were armed, and to accompany operations on land in which artillery might be employed, such as the rockets in the War of 1812. They were permitted to purchase blue jackets and overalls for work and service, to preserve their ordinary uniform, and in 1811 they were authorised to wear a blue uniform like that of the Royal Artillery, but with distinctive insignia.

A PRIVATE of the ROYAL MARINES.

PLATE 54
Cadets of the Royal Military College at Sandhurst, Junior Department
(published January 1813)

One of the most famous of all military instructional institutions, the Royal Military Academy at Sandhurst was a relatively new formation when Hamilton Smith executed this plate. An academy had been established at Woolwich in 1741 for the instruction of cadets in artillery and engineering, but no wider institution existed for the training of regimental or staff officers. This need was recognised by John Gaspard Le Marchant (1766–1812), one of the most intelligent and innovative officers of his generation, who had designed the 1796 cavalry sabres and had devised the drill that went with them. His experiences on campaign convinced him of the need to improve the education and training of officers, and his original concept was for a college of three departments: junior, for cadets aged 13–15; second, to finish the education of older youths in preparation for a commission; and senior, a staff college for officers of at least four years' service.

His plan, which was supported in principle by the Duke of York, coincided with the establishment in 1799 of what was virtually a private school for the training of staff officers, by the French émigré General François Jarry de Vrigny de la Villette (1733–1807) at High Wycombe. Trained as a staff officer under Frederick the Great, Jarry was an ideal tutor and collaborator with Le Marchant, and his school was accepted as an official institution by a Warrant of 24 June 1801, with Le Marchant named as lieutenant-governor of the 'Royal Military College'.

In March 1802 the Junior Department was authorised, with the intention of providing an education for those who intended to become officers, or for the sons of fallen, disabled or impecunious officers, who might not otherwise be able to afford such an education. Of the initial intake of 100 cadets, 30 were of the latter category, receiving free education; 30 were the sons of gentlemen, 20 were cadets of the East India Company service who paid £90 per annum, and 20 the sons of serving officers, paying £40 per annum. (To prevent discrimination, no cadet was permitted to enter the College with more than one guinea in his possession, or to receive more than 2s 6d pocket money per week.) The cadets were organised as a company, with four of their number appointed as officers and five as sergeants (note the rank-markings on the left sleeve of the seated figure). Although under the same authority as the senior department, the junior was based originally at Great Marlow, but from 1808 it was decided to construct a new establishment at Sandhurst, with the number of cadets increased to four companies.

Le Marchant was not to see the fulfilment of the scheme; when he was promoted to major-general in June 1811 it was said that his position there was not appropriate for his enhanced rank, and he went instead to the Peninsula, dying in circumstances of great gallantry leading his cavalry at Salamanca. Although the College had relatively limited effect in the officers it produced before the end of the Napoleonic Wars, it was to become one of the great centres of military learning and excellence. Hamilton Smith's plate shows the dress of the cadets, the NCO carrying a sword instead of the musket and cross belts of the others, while the central figure wears an undress cap. They are shown as young men, cadets entering the college between the ages of 13 and 15.

CADETS

of the ROYAL MILITARY COLLEGE *at* SANDHURST,

JUNIOR DEPARTMENT.

PLATE 55
Children of the Royal Military Asylum, Chelsea
(published August 1813)

This most unusual of Hamilton Smith's plates depicts the 'uniform' of the children of the Royal Military Asylum. This 'Asylum for educating one thousand children, the legal offspring of British soldiers' was based at Chelsea, in the location later known as the Duke of York's Headquarters. The creation of the Duke of York, when Commander-in-Chief, it was modelled to an extent upon the Royal Hibernian Military School, founded in Dublin in 1769 for the orphans of soldiers on the Irish establishment. The Duke laid its foundation stone on 19 June 1801, and it opened in 1803 as a free boarding school for the orphans and other children of NCOs and private soldiers. Preference for admission was given to orphans; then to those whose fathers had died on service; and thirdly to those whose mothers had died and whose fathers were serving abroad. Hitherto, regimental depots had been caring for many such children. From 150 inmates at the opening in 1803, the number rose to 1,200 by 1811, and the institution took over a similar establishment operating in the Isle of Wight, which was used to care for the very youngest infants.

The Asylum was open to both boys and girls (for boys only after 1840), who received a reasonable standard of conventional education, plus military subjects like drill, physical exercise and gunnery, and 'handicrafts' like shoemaking or tailoring, which would have been of especial use if the boys from the Asylum subsequently joined the army. (This was obviously encouraged, but it was not a condition of entry that they should.) The teaching of such handicrafts not only economised upon the upkeep of the institution, the children making their own clothes and shoes, but they were even able to sell some of their products to help finances. In 1892 the name of the institution was changed to The Duke of York's Royal Military School, and in 1909 it moved to Dover.

The Duke took great interest in the school, which was a typical expression of his care; justifiably, he was known in the army as 'The Soldier's Friend'. An example of his charity was provided by the case of the McMullen family. Private Peter McMullen of the 27th Foot was terribly wounded at Waterloo, losing both arms; his pregnant wife, Elizabeth, remained with the battalion during the battle until she was wounded in the leg while assisting an injured soldier. On their return home a child was born at the York Hospital, Chelsea; she was named (after the Duke of York) 'Frederica McMullen of Waterloo', and the Duke himself stood as her godfather. For all the Duke's concern, however, the child survived only until December 1815.

As appropriate for a 'Royal' institution, the uniform worn by the children included blue facings to their red jackets. Such was the military nature of the establishment that some children were appointed as NCOs, like the little girl shown wearing corporal's chevrons. The uniform was largely unchanged when Alexandre-Jean Dubois Drahonet painted portraits of some inmates for King William IV in 1832, though by this time a rather more elaborate forage cap with a flat top and red band was used, and apparently old 1812 shakos for 'dress' occasions.[1]

1. See Spencer-Smith, J., *Portraits for a King*, London 1990.

CHILDREN

of the ROYAL MILITARY ASYLUM, CHELSEA.

PLATE 56

Chelsea Pensioners, Cavalry & Infantry

(published November 1814)

The Royal Hospital, Chelsea, was established by King Charles II in 1681 as a home for poor, injured ex-soldiers. He laid the foundation stone in the following year, although it was a decade before the first 'in-pensioners' were admitted to the institution, the building for which was designed by Sir Christopher Wren. Although able to accommodate a maximum of about 500 men, it also acted as the administrative centre for the payment of army pensions.

A pension was not the automatic right of all discharged soldiers, but those who had been injured or incapacitated as a result of their duties, or who had 20 years' service, might apply to become an 'out-pensioner' in receipt of a Chelsea pension. Pensions were paid in cash, in advance, every three months, by the Collector of Excise of each district, to whom the pensioner had to apply for his money. The number of ex-soldiers who received army pensions was considerable, rising from 20,150 in 1792 to more than 61,000 by 1819 and to more than 85,000 by 1828, Chelsea having in 1822 taken over the responsibility for paying the 15,000 pensioners previously paid by the equivalent institution in Ireland, the hospital at Kilmainham. Pensioners who were physically able to join a Veteran Battalion (units which had replaced the old companies of Invalids) would forfeit their pension if they refused to serve if required.

The sum paid to pensioners varied with their level of incapacity and their rank when they left the army. In 1814, for example, it was stated that a 1st class pension was £18 5s *per annum*, 2nd class 13 guineas, and 3rd class £7 12s (which equated to 1s, almost 9d and almost 5d *per diem* respectively). For blindness or the loss of a limb, a sergeant's pension was 1s 6d per day, a corporal's 1s 2d, and a private's 1s, and for the loss of more than one limb, or incapacitation to prevent the earning of any living, the sums were not to exceed 3s 6d, 3s and 2s 6d respectively. While these sums were not inconsiderable when compared with a soldier's daily pay, in most cases they were inadequate for the maintenance of civilian life: in the post-Waterloo period, for example, when a textile worker might earn more than a guinea a week, the average pension was 1s 5d per day, almost a quarter of out-pensioners received only 3s 6d per week, and more than another quarter only 5s 3d per week (6d and 9d per day respectively).

Such sums were markedly less than pensions awarded to wounded officers, although their pensions were granted only for severe injuries which might not necessarily be incapacitating. For example, Lieutenant John Browne of the 4th Foot was in receipt of a pension of £70 for an injury sustained at Badajoz, when he was wounded even more severely at Waterloo, for which he received a further £100 pension (although the latter was for a serious head injury, he survived until 1849).

The Chelsea 'in-pensioners', however, were somewhat more fortunate, and as may be seen from this plate, they wore a uniform not very dissimilar to that worn to this day, and which even in 1814 was considerably old-fashioned.

Note: For those unfamiliar with values of pre-decimal currency: 1d = 0.5p approx, 1s = 5p, 1 guinea = £1 1s = £1.05. Alternatively there were 12 (old) pence (d) to the shilling (s) and 20 shillings to the pound.

CHELSEA PENSIONERS,

CAVALRY & INFANTRY.

Troops of the
East India Company

PLATE 57

Native Troops E[ast] India Company's Service:
Troops of the Bodyguard of the Gov[erno]r General [L], Private of the Bengal Regular Cavalry [Centre], Private of the Java Volunteers [R]
(published March 1815)

The regular cavalry maintained by the three Indian Presidencies, like the infantry, wore a combination of European uniform and items based upon Indian styles, most notably in the design of head-dress. In most other respects, arms and equipment were similar to those used in British service.

Although there had been a small bodyguard for the commander-in-chief between 1762 and 1772, the Governor-General's Bodyguard originated in 1773 and continued in existence after Indian independence as the President's Bodyguard. Red coats appear to have been worn at least from the late 18th century, and the light dragoon style is shown in illustrations from the early 19th century. The uniform shown by Hamilton Smith is in British light dragoon style pre-1812, with white braid, with a bulbous blue 'turban' trimmed with white lace and a white tuft. Officers and European NCOs wore helmets, presumably the 'Tarleton' which certainly had been in use *c.* 1805. An undress uniform in use at the date of this plate included blue linen jackets, cossa or muslin turbans, and pantaloons of 'dosooty', a coarse, double-threaded cotton.

Details of the history of the Bengal Native Cavalry are given in the Introduction (p. 29). Initially their uniforms were red, like that of the Bodyguard, with white lace and facings of blue, yellow, white, green, buff, orange, yellow and yellow for the 1st–8th regiments respectively, the 6th changing from orange to grey facings in 1808 presumably to make a greater contrast with the red jacket. In December 1809 it was ordered that the jackets be changed to French grey with red facings and white lace for all, but in the following March the facing colour was changed to orange; although the difficulty in procuring French grey cloth meant that the change was not completed until 1811. It is this uniform that is shown in this plate, with the blue bulbous 'turban', and also in the appropriate chart (Plate 60). Like the Bodyguard, the Native Cavalry undress uniform at this period included blue linen jackets and dosooty pantaloons.

The Java Volunteers, or Java Hussars, were formed in 1812, following the British occupation of that island. Two troops in strength, the unit was commanded by Captain L.H. O'Brien of the Madras Cavalry, and was disbanded when Java reverted to Dutch control in 1816. Hamilton Smith shows its uniform in light cavalry style like the others in this plate, in blue with yellow facings and white lace, and a red turban. The man shown carries the 1796 pattern light cavalry sabre, with which the Bengal Native Cavalry evidently was armed from 1803. The equipment of the men illustrated is similarly of British cavalry style.

NATIVE TROOPS E. INDIA COMPANY'S SERVICE.

1. TROOPS of the BODY GUARD of the GOVᴿ GENERAL.

2. PRIVATE of the BENGAL REGULAR CAVALRY.

3. PRIVATE of the JAVA VOLUNTEERS.

Aquatinted by I.C.Stadler.

PLATE 58

Native Troops, E[ast] India Company's Service:
A Serjeant of Light Infantry, and Private of Madrass [sic] Sepoys
(published March 1815)

The organisation and origin of the Madras Infantry are described in the Introduction (p. 29).

As with the Native Cavalry, by the late 18th century the uniform of the Native Infantry in part resembled that of the equivalent British troops. The red infantry jacket was like the British pattern, except that the skirts were ordered to 'slope off' from the hips, evidently without turnbacks, with standing collars ordered from 1802. Shoulder straps and wings were as for British battalion and flank companies respectively. The facing colours borne upon the collar, cuffs and shoulder straps were specified in 1801 as white (1st and 15th Regiments), green (2nd), red (3rd and 10th), orange (4th), black (5th and 14th), buff (6th and 19th), French grey (7th), bright yellow (8th), gosling green (9th), pale buff (11th), willow green (12th), philemot yellow (13th), pale yellow (16th), deep yellow (17th) and Saxon blue (18th). Regiments raised subsequently were the 20th (1804, green), 21st (1804, bright yellow), 22nd (1804, pale yellow), 23rd (1804, white), 24th (1807, pale buff), and 25th (1807, bright yellow, though Plate 60 appears to show white). In 1801 it was specified that the lace loops should be in pairs (evenly-spaced for the 3rd, 6th, 13th and 17th), but Plate 60 shows evenly-spaced for all.

An obvious difference between this uniform and that of the British infantry was in the head-dress. Prior to 1797 flat bonnets had been worn, but then a bell-topped turban with sloping top was introduced, made of blue cloth around a bamboo framework, with yellow lace decoration. A new pattern was decreed in November 1805, including a plume and leather cockade, but its resemblance to a shako (regarded as a Christian head-dress) aroused great unease among the troops. Although it was not the only cause of the terrible mutiny at Vellore in 1806, the fear that it heralded a process of forcible change of religion was one of the contributory reasons, and in July 1806 the 1797 pattern, as shown here, was reinstated.

Other similarities with British infantry uniform shown here include the rank markings (sergeants' sash with facing-coloured stripe and the chevrons which replaced the previous shoulder-knots in 1806) and equipment. The traditional legwear of shorts (*janghirs* or *jangeers*) were replaced by pantaloons for full dress and garrison wear from February 1812, but the colour was not regulated: plain or striped material was permitted as each regiment preferred, providing that the colour did not look out of place with the jacket or facings; and not until 1812 was a uniform pattern of sandal ordered.

As shown here, four battalions were converted to light infantry in 1812 – the 1/3rd, 1/12th, 1/16th and 2/17th – which became the Palamcottah, Wallajahbad, Trinchinopoly and Chicacole Light Infantry respectively. In November 1812 it was ordered that they should all have dark green facings as illustrated (though pointed cuffs were specified), white lace with a green stripe, and coloured pantaloons (white for hot weather, apparently red at other times, and black specified in January 1816). They are also recorded as carrying Baker rifles, with black equipment and powder horns.

C.H.S.

Aquatinted by I.C.Stadler.

NATIVE TROOPS, E. INDIA COMPANYS SERVICE.

A SERJEANT of LIGHT INFANTRY, and PRIVATE of MADRASS SEPOYS.

Plate 59

Native Troops, E[ast] India Company's Service:
A Serjeant and a Private Grenadier Sepoy of the Bengal Army
(published March 1815)

The history and organisation of the Bengal Infantry are covered in the Introduction (p. 29).

As mentioned in the text to Plate 58, the uniform of the Native Infantry resembled that of the British in a number of ways. Initially, mixed facing colours were worn, but in 1809 all regiments of the Bengal Infantry were ordered to wear yellow facings, white buttons and lace striped red, white and blue. (The Marine regiment, formed 1795 and with a second battalion raised in 1802, which became the 1/ and 2/20th Regiments in 1803, was ordered to retain its blue facings and yellow lace in 1809, although Plate 60 shows it with the universal yellow facings.)

The jacket shown in this plate resembles that of the British infantry, but it appears that the Bengal Infantry may have been very slow in adopting this style, with the old open-fronted coat with lapels perhaps being retained as late as 1811. Both men illustrated have the wings of a flank company in British style, and the sergeant has a British-style sash with facing coloured stripe, and a short sword. He appears to carry no musket, and has no cartridge box belt, nor does he carry a spontoon, which was only abolished for *havildars* (sergeants) of the Bengal Native Infantry in 1831. (Sergeants of light companies usually carried fusils, and perhaps those of grenadiers as well.) Originally the long pantaloons were restricted to native officers, but their use was extended to *havildars* in 1801, and after that some units wore them in cold weather. In June 1813 permission was granted for the use of pantaloons all year, if units chose to wear them in preference to the traditional shorts (*janghirs*). The traditional style of the latter, as worn by the Bengal Infantry had a pattern of blue triangles around the bottom edge, as here, and were considerably shorter than those worn by the Madras Infantry (see Plate 58).

The head-dress of the Bengal Infantry had been a large, flat-brimmed hat sometimes styled a 'sundial hat', but from 1805 bell-topped turbans were worn, or cloth on a framework of rattan, and although Hamilton Smith shows only the lace band and yellow ornaments, other contemporary illustrations depict the use of various badges, including regimental numbers or inscription, a wreath (for battalion companies?), and a grenade or bugle-horn badge inside a wreath for grenadiers and light companies (formed in 1808) respectively. Metal ornaments were permitted. As shown here and in Plate 58, Native Infantry did not wear leather stocks around the neck like the British, but white neck-cloths, and in Bengal especially, beads around the neck were popular. From 1796 the equipment of the Bengal Infantry was ordered to be black, but from 1810 gradual replacement with white leather was sanctioned.

Apparently some regiments customarily wore some form of undress uniform on active service, for in May 1805 Lieutenant John Pester compared other regiments with his own:

> 'Their clothes had been worn only on parade duties, whilst our men's regimentals had been soiled with gunpowder and dirt in the trenches, to which they had been accustomed without intermission for the last five months. Nor were they a little proud of their rags and tatters, and assured their smarter friends that they wore their *fighting* coats.'[1]

1. Pester, J., *War and Sport in India 1802–1806: An Officer's Diary*, London, n.d. (1913), p. 405.

C.H.S.

NATIVE TROOPS E. INDIA COMPANYS SERVICE,

A SERJEANT and a PRIVATE GRENADIER SEPOY of the BENGAL ARMY.

PLATE 60

Facings of the Honourable United East India Company's Regular Army, January 1814

Details of the armies of the three Presidencies are given in the Introduction (pp. 28–29) and in the texts to Plates 57–59, but only in this plate are there any illustrations of the Bombay Army. Details of the history and organisation of the Bombay Infantry are noted in the Introduction (p. 29), and their uniform charts are shown here. Their uniforms were similar to those of Madras and Bengal, with universally yellow facings by 1792, until regimental facing colours were adopted (by 1812): light red or orange, light blue, black, white, popinjay green, light yellow or buff, pea green, 'pompadour' (purple-blue) and pale yellow for the 1st–9th Regiments respectively. The infantry jacket was worn with *janghirs* decorated with blue like those shown in Plates 58–59, but mid-way in length between those of the Madras and Bengal patterns. The head-dress was a curious construction mid-way between a grenadier's mitre cap and a bulbous turban with a front-plate and a ball at the top; originally worn just by grenadiers, from 1796 it was ordered that all should have a brass front-plate on their head-dress, bearing the regimental number. After about 1814 the head-dress came to resemble a dark blue, peakless shako with chin-scales, the regimental number on the front and a plume or ball. The unbecoming nature of the Bombay Native Infantry's head-dress at this time gave rise to their nickname, bestowed by the Bengal Army, of '*untoo-googras*', made up from the words for 'ball' and for the bowl of a hookah respectively, which it was said the head-dress resembled! It was recorded that one regiment was given a nickname from an attempt by its colonel's lady to make it appear more European by providing it with ruffled shirts, after which the unit became known as the '*Ruffledar-ki-Pultan*' ('the Ruffle-Wearing Regiment'), until the ruffles were laughed out of use![1]

In addition to the numbered infantry regiments, a Bombay Marine Battalion existed from January 1777, and became the 1st Battalion of a new 11th Regiment in January 1818. Although the men wore a blue working dress, their full dress is shown here, the red infantry uniform with green facings, and an appropriate anchor device upon the head-dress plate.

As mentioned in the Introduction (p. 28), all three Presidencies maintained regiments of European infantry, which like the European officers of the Native regiments, wore uniforms and equipment of entirely European style. Unlike the British infantry charts, Hamilton Smith shows no lace for the European units. The Bengal European Regiment had adopted yellow facings *c.* 1803, and in 1809 it was ordered that its lace should have red and blue stripes. For the Madras Europeans, light blue facings were specified in 1799, but by 1810 they were described as 'French grey' (conceivably the same shade as before), the other ranks' lace with yellow, scarlet and black stripes. For the Bombay Europeans, the facing colour had been yellow from May 1792. For the Indian artillery and engineers, see the Introduction (pp. 28–29).

---

1. See Cadell, Sir Patrick, 'The Dress of the Bombay Soldier', in *Journal of the Society for Army Historical Research*, Vol. XXVI (1949), pp. 144–45.

FACINGS OF THE HONOURABLE UNITED EAST INDIA COMPANYS
REGULAR ARMY
JAN.Y 1814.

BENGAL NATIVE CAVALRY.

BENGAL INFANTRY &c.

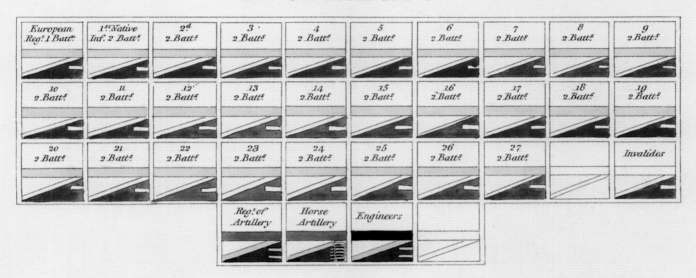

MADRASS NATIVE CAVALRY.

MADRASS INFANTRY &c.

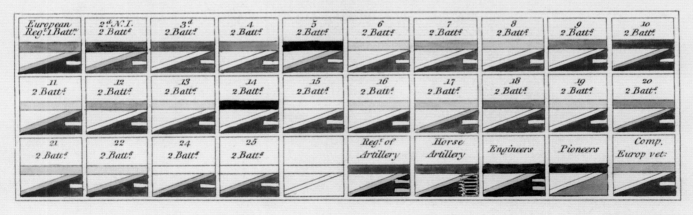

BOMBAY INFANTRY &c.

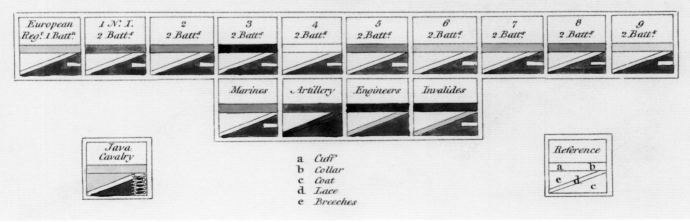

Java Cavalry

Reference
a Cuff
b Collar
c Coat
d Lace
e Breeches

Regiments of the British Army 1814–15

The following lists the regiments of the British Army in order of seniority, at the time they were depicted by Hamilton Smith, with the colonels listed for the period 1814–15 (their names and titles as given in 1814). Details are also included of changes of regimental titles which occurred during the Napoleonic Wars. The Royal Regiment of Artillery and Corps of Royal Engieneers appear in their traditional place in the order of seniority, although at the time they and other elements of the Ordnance were placed at the end of the *Army List*.

1st Life Guards Gen. Earl of Harrington

2nd Life Guards Gen. Earl Cathcart

Royal Horse Guards (Blue)
  Field Marshal Duke of Wellington

1st (King's) Dragoon Guards Gen. Sir David Dundas

2nd (Queen's) Dragoon Guards
  Lt. Gen. Sir Charles Craufurd

3rd (Prince of Wales's) Dragoon Guards
  Gen. Richard Vyse

4th (Royal Irish) Dragoon Guards Lt. Gen. Miles Staveley; from 3 August 1814, Maj. Gen. Sir Henry Fane

5th (Princess Charlotte of Wales's) Dragoon Guards *(titled Princess Charlotte's from 1804)* Gen. Thomas Bland

6th Dragoon Guards (Carabiniers) Gen. Earl Carhampton

7th (Princess Royal's) Dragoon Guards
  Gen. Richard Wilford

1st (Royal) Dragoons Gen. Thomas Garth

2nd (Royal North British) Dragoons *(known as Royal Scots Greys)* General Marquess Lothian; from 12 January 1815, Gen. Sir James Steuart

3rd (King's Own) Dragoons Lt. Gen. William Cartwright

4th (Queen's Own) Dragoons Lt. Gen. Francis Hugonin

6th (Inniskilling) Dragoons Gen. Earl of Pembroke

7th (Queen's Own) Light Dragoons (Hussars) *(Hussars from 1806)* Lt. Gen. Earl of Uxbridge

8th (King's Royal Irish) Light Dragoons Gen. John Floyd

9th Light Dragoons Lt. Gen. Earl Rosslyn

10th (Prince of Wales's Own Royal) Light Dragoons (Hussars) *(Hussars from 1806; 'Prince of Wales's Own' until 1811, when title 'Royal' added)* Prince Regent

11th Light Dragoons Lt. Gen. Lord William Bentinck

12th (Prince of Wales's) Light Dragoons
  Gen. Sir James Steuart Denham; from 12 January 1815, Lt. Gen. Sir William Payne Bt.

13th Light Dragoons Lt. Gen. Hon. Sir Henry Grey

14th (Duchess of York's Own) Light Dragoons *('Duchess of York's Own' from 1798)* Gen. Earl of Bridgwater

15th (King's) Light Dragoons (Hussars) *(Hussars from 1806)* Field Marshal Duke of Cumberland

16th (Queen's) Light Dragoons Gen. Earl Harcourt

17th Light Dragoons Gen. Oliver De Lancey

18th (King's) Light Dragoons (Hussars) *(Hussars from 1807)* Gen. Marquess of Drogheda

19th Light Dragoons Maj. Gen. John Vandeleur

20th Light Dragoons *(titled Jamaica Light Dragoons until 1802)* Lt. Gen. Lord Combermere

21st Light Dragoons *(raised 1794)* Gen. Banastre Tarleton

22nd Light Dragoons *(raised 1794, numbered 25th until 1802)* Gen. Francis E. Gwyn

23rd Light Dragoons *(raised 1795; numbered 26th until 1802)* Lt. Gen. Sir William Payne Bt.; from 3 August 1814, Maj. Gen. Sir George Anson

24th Light Dragoons *(raised 1795; numbered 27th until 1802)* Gen. William Loftus

25th Light Dragoons *(raised 1795; numbered 29th until 1802)* Lt. Gen. Lord Charles W. Stewart

Royal Regiment of Artillery Gen. Earl of Mulgrave*

Invalid Battn, Royal Artillery
  Colonel-Commandant: Maj. Gen. R. Douglas

Corps of Royal Engineers
  Colonel-in-Chief: Gen. Earl of Mulgrave*

Staff Corps of Cavalry
  Major-Commandant: Lt. Col. George Scovell

Royal Waggon Train
  Colonel-Commandant: Maj. Gen. Digby Hamilton

1st Foot Guards Field Marshal Duke of York

2nd (Coldstream) Foot Guards
  Field Marshal Duke of Cambridge

3rd (Scots) Foot Guards Gen. Duke of Gloucester

1st (Royal Scots) Regt Field Marshal Duke of Kent

2nd (Queen's Royal) Regt Gen. James Coates

3rd (East Kent) Regt or Buffs Gen. Charles Leigh

4th (King's Own) Regt Gen. Earl of Chatham

5th (Northumberland) Regt Lt. Gen. William Wynyard

6th (1st Warwickshire) Regt Gen. Sir George Nugent Bt.

7th (Royal) Fuzileers Gen. Sir Alured Clarke

8th (King's) Regt Gen. Edmund Stevens

9th (East Norfolk) Regt Gen. Robert Brownrigg

10th (North Lincoln) Regt
  Lt. Gen. Hon. Thomas Maitland

11th (North Devon) Regt Gen. Sir Charles Asgill Bt.

12th (East Suffolk) Regt Gen. Sir Charles Hastings Bt.

13th (1st Somersetshire) Regt Gen. Edward Morrison

14th (Buckinghamshire) Regt *('Bedfordshire' until 1809)* Lt. Gen. Sir Harry Calvert

15th (York East Riding) Regt Gen. Henry W. Powell; from 23 July 1814, Lt. Gen. Sir Moore Disney

16th (Bedfordshire) Regt *('Buckinghamshire' until 1809)* Lt. Gen. Sir George Prevost Bt.

17th (Leicestershire) Regt Gen. George Garth

18th (Royal Irish) Regt Gen. Lord Hutchinson

19th (1st York North Riding) Regt
  Lt. Gen. Tomkins H. Turner

20th (East Devonshire) Regt Lt. Gen. Sir John Stuart; from 5 April 1815, Lt. Gen. Sir William Houston

21st (Royal North British) Fuzileers
  Gen. Hon. William Gordon

22nd (Cheshire) Regt Lt. Gen. Hon Edward Finch

23rd (Royal Welch) Fuzileers Gen. Richard Grenville

24th (2nd Warwickshire) Regt Gen. Sir David Baird Bt.

25th (King's Own Borderers) *('Sussex' until 1805)* Lt. Gen. Hon. Charles Fitzroy

26th (Cameronian) Regt Lt. Gen. Earl of Dalhousie

27th (Inniskilling) Regt Gen. Earl of Moira

28th (North Gloucestershire) Regt Gen. Robert Prescott; from 26 December 1815, Gen. Hon. Sir Edward Paget

29th (Worcestershire) Regt Gen. Gordon Forbes

30th (Cambridgeshire) Regt Gen. Robert Manners

31st (Huntingdonshire) Regt Gen. Earl of Mulgrave*

32nd (Cornwall) Regt Gen. Alexander Campbell

33rd (1st York West Riding) Regt
  Lt. Gen. Sir John Sherbrooke

* Although an individual could hold only one Army colonelcy, Gen. the Earl of Mulgrave was colonel of the 31st Foot, and the RA and RE, but the latter two posts were held by virtue of his appointment as Master-General of the Ordnance.

34th (Cumberland) Regt Gen. Sir Eyre Coote

35th (Sussex) Regt *('Dorsetshire' until 1805)*
Gen. Duke of Richmond

36th (Hertfordshire) Regt Gen. Hon. Henry St John

37th (North Hampshire) Regt Lt. Gen. Sir Charles Green

38th (1st Staffordshire) Regt Gen. Earl Ludlow

39th (Dorsetshire) Regt *('East Middlesex' until 1807)*
Gen. Nisbet Balfour

40th (2nd Somersetshire) Regt
Gen. Sir George Osborn Bt.

41st Regt Lt. Gen. Josiah Champagne

42nd (Royal Highland) Regt *(known as Black Watch)*
Lt. Gen. Marquess of Huntly

43rd (Monmouthshire) Light Infantry *(light infantry from 1803)* Gen. Sir John Cradock

44th (East Essex) Regt Gen. Earl of Suffolk

45th (Nottinghamshire) Regt
Gen. Frederick Cavendish Lister

46th (South Devonshire) Regt Gen. John Whyte

47th (Lancashire) Regt Lt. Gen. Hon. Sir Alexander Hope

48th (Northamptonshire) Regt Gen. Lord Charles Fitzroy

49th (Hertfordshire) Regt Gen. Hon. Alexander Maitland

50th (West Kent) Regt Gen. Sir James Duff

51st (2nd York West Riding) Light Infantry *(light infantry from 1809)* Gen. William Morshead

52nd (Oxfordshire) Light Infantry *(light infantry from 1809)* Lt. Gen. Sir Hildebrand Oakes Bt.

53rd (Shropshire) Regt Lt. Gen. Hon. John Abercromby

54th (West Norfolk) Regt Lt. Gen. James, Lord Forbes

55th (Westmoreland) Regt Lt. Gen. William Clinton

56th (West Essex) Regt Gen. Hon. Chapple Norton

57th (West Middlesex) Regt Gen. Sir Hew Dalrymple

58th (Rutlandshire) Regt Gen. Earl of Cavan

59th (2nd Nottinghamshire) Regt Gen. Alexander Ross

60th (Royal American) Regt
Colonel-in-Chief: Field Marshal Duke of York
Battalion colonels. 1st: Lt. Gen. Sir Henry Clinton (from 9 August 1815, Lt. Gen. Sir Wroth Acland); *2nd:* Gen. Thomas Carleton; *3rd:* Lt. Gen. Hon. Sir Edmund Phipps; *4th:* Lt. Gen. Hon. Charles Hope; *5th:* Lt. Gen. John Robinson; *6th:* Gen. Napier Burton; *7th:* Maj. Gen. Sir George Murray; *8th:* Maj. Gen. James Kempt

61st (South Gloucestershire) Regt
Gen. Sir George Hewitt Bt.

62nd (Wiltshire) Regt Gen. Samuel Hulse

63rd (West Suffolk) Regt Gen. Earl of Balcarres

64th (2nd Staffordshire) Regt Lt. Gen. Henry Wynyard

65th (2nd York North Riding) Regt
Lt. Gen. Thomas Grosvenor

66th (Berkshire) Regt Gen. Oliver Nicolls

67th (South Hampshire) Regt Gen. Sir William Keppel

68th (Durham) Light Infantry *(light infantry from 1808)*
Lt. Gen. Henry Warde

69th (South Lincolnshire) Regt
Gen. Sir Cornelius Cuyler Bt.

70th (Glasgow Lowland) Regt *('Surrey' until 1812)*
Lt. Gen. Hon. Sir Galbraith Lowry Cole

71st (Highland) Light Infantry *('Glasgow Highland' 1808-10; light infantry from 1809)* Gen. Francis Dundas

72nd (Highland) Regt Gen. James Stuart;
from 29 April 1815, Lt. Gen. Rowland, Lord Hill

73rd Regt *('Highland' until 1809)* Gen. George Harris

74th (Highland) Regt Lt. Gen. James Montgomerie

75th Regt *('Highland' until 1809)*
Gen. Sir Robert Abercromby

76th Regt *('Hindoostan Regt' 1807-12)*
Lt. Gen. Christopher Chowne

77th (East Middlesex) Regt Lt. Gen. Sir Thomas Picton;
from 23 June 1815, Lt. Gen. Sir George Cooke

78th (Highland) Regt or Ross-shire Buffs *(raised 1793)*
Lt. Gen. Sir Samuel Auchmuty

79th (Cameron) Highlanders *(raised 1793; 'Cameronian Volunteers' until 1804)* Maj. Gen. Sir Alan Cameron

80th (Staffordshire Volunteers) *(raised 1793)*
Lt. Gen. Hon. Sir Edward Paget;
from 26 Dec. 1815, Lt. Gen. Sir Alexander Campbell Bt.

81st Regt *(raised 1793; 'Loyal Lincolnshire Villagers' until 1794)* Gen. Henry Johnson

82nd (Prince of Wales's Volunteers) *(raised 1793)*
Gen. Henry Pigot

83rd Regt *(raised 1793)* Gen. James Balfour

84th (York and Lancaster) Regt *(raised 1793, titled 'York and Lancaster' from 1809)* Gen. George Bernard

85th (Bucks Volunteers) Light Infantry *(raised 1793; light infantry from 1808)* Gen. Thomas S. Stanwix

86th (Royal County Down) Regt *(raised 1793; titled 'Leinster' 1809-12)* Gen. Hon. Francis Needham

87th (Prince of Wales's Own Irish) *(raised 1793, 'Prince of Wales's Irish' until 1811)* Lt. Gen. Sir John Doyle Bt.

88th (Connaught Rangers) *(raised 1793)*
Lt. Gen. Lord Beresford

89th Regt *(raised 1794)* Gen. Earl of Lindsey

90th (Perthshire Volunteers) *(raised 1794)*
Lt. Gen. Lord Lynedoch

91st Regt *(raised 1794; numbered 98th until 1798; 'Argyllshire Highlanders' until 1809)*
Lt. Gen. Duncan Campbell of Lochnell

92nd (Highland) Regt *(known as Gordon Highlanders; raised 1794, numbered 100th until 1798)*
Lt. Gen. Lord Niddery

93rd (Highland) Regt *(known as Sutherland Highlanders; raised 1800)* Gen. William Wemyss of Wemyss

94th (Scotch Brigade) *(raised 1685 but only brought into the line in 1802)* Lt. Gen. Rowland, Lord Hill;
from 29 April 1815, Maj. Gen. Sir Charles Colville

95th Rifle Corps *(raised 1800, numbered 95th 1803)*
Colonel-in-Chief: Gen. Sir David Dundas
Battalion colonels. 1st: Lt. Gen. Forbes Champagne;
2nd: Lt. Gen. Sir Brent Spencer;
3rd: Lt. Gen. Hon. Sir William Stewart

96th Regt *(raised 1798 as 2nd Battn 52nd, numbered 96th from 1802)* Gen. George Don

97th (Queens Own German) *(Minorca Regt, retitled Queen's German Regt, numbered 97th from 1804)*
Lt. Gen. Gordon Drummond

98th Regt *(raised 1804)* Col. John Burke

99th (Prince of Wales's Tipperary) Regt *(raised 1804, titled thus from 1811)* Lt. Gen. Hon. H. Mathew

100th (Prince Regent's County of Dublin) Regt *(raised 1805, titled thus from 1812)* Col. Sir Frederick John Falkiner Bt.

101st (Duke of York's Irish) Regt *(raised 1806)*
Col. Henry, Viscount Dillon

102nd Regt *(New South Wales Corps taken into the line and numbered 102nd in 1808)*
Lt. Gen. Sir A. Gledstanes

103rd Regt *(9th Garrison Battn until 1808)*
Lt. Gen. George Porter

104th Regt *(New Brunswick Fencibles taken into the line and numbered 104th in 1811)* Lt. Gen. M. Hunter

Royal Staff Corps Maj. Gen. J. Brown

1st West India Regt Gen. Lord Charles Somerset
2nd West India Regt Gen. Sir George Beckwith
3rd West India Regt Lt. Gen. Sir John Murray Bt.
4th West India Regt Lt. Gen. Sir James Leith
5th West India Regt Gen. J. Despard
6th West India Regt
Maj. Gen. Hon. Sir Edward Pakenham;
from 20 March 1815, Lt. Gen. Sir Miles Nightingall
7th West India Regt Lt. Gen. Isaac Gascoyne
8th West India Regt Lt. Gen. Sir Thomas Hislop Bt.
Royal African Corps Maj. Gen. James Willoughby Gordon
Royal York Rangers Lt. Gen. J. Fraser

Royal West India Rangers Lt. Gen. Hon. William Lumley

York Chasseurs Maj. Gen. Hugh M. Gordon

1st Ceylon Regt Lt. Gen. Frederick Maitland

2nd Ceylon Regt Lt. Gen. Sir John Hamilton

3rd Ceylon Regt Lt. Gen. William Thomas

4th Ceylon Regt Maj. Gen. John Wilson

Cape Regt Lt. Gen. G. Moncrieffe

Bourbon Regt Lt. Col. Commandant: Col. H.S. Keating

1st Garrison Battn *(disbanded Dec. 1814)*
Lt. Gen. George Vansittart

2nd Garrison Battn *(disbanded Dec. 1814)*
Lt. Col. George Porter;
from 12 January 1814, Maj. Gen. Frederick P. Robinson

3rd Garrison Battn *(re-numbered as 1st, Dec. 1814)*
Lt. Gen. Baldwin Leighton;
(3rd Battn re-formed May 1815) Lt. Gen. John Hodgson

4th Garrison Battn *(re-numbered as 2nd, Dec. 1814)*
Lt. Gen. William Houston;
from 5 April 1815, Maj. Gen. Henry Torrens

5th Garrison Battn *(disbanded Dec. 1814)*
Maj. Gen. Hon. Charles Colville

6th Garrison Battn *(disbanded Dec. 1814)*
Maj. Gen. Gore Browne

1st Royal Veteran Battn *(disbanded July 1814)*
Gen. James Stewart;
(re-formed Aug. 1815) no colonel appointed

2nd Royal Veteran Battn *(disbanded Sept. 1814–Jan. 1815)*
Lt.Gen Anthony L. Layard;
(re-formed June 1815) Gen. John W.T. Watson

3rd Royal Veteran Battn *(disbanded July 1814)*
Gen. William Maxwell;
(re-formed June 1815) Gen. Sir Paulus A. Irving, Bt.

4th Royal Veteran Battn *(disbanded Sept. 1814)*
Gen. Grice Blakeney

5th Royal Veteran Battn *(disbanded July 1814)*
Lt. Gen. John M. Kerr;
(re-formed June 1815) Gen. Andrew J. Drummond

6th (Royal North British) Veteran Battn *(disbanded July 1814)* Gen. Sir Paulus A. Irving Bt.;
(re-formed June 1815) no colonel appointed.

7th Royal Veteran Battn *(disbanded Aug. 1814)*
Gen. Thomas Murray

8th Royal Veteran Battn *(disbanded July 1814)*
Gen. W.T. Watson;
(re-formed June 1815) Col. Alexander Mair

9th Royal Veteran Battn *(disbanded July–Aug. 1814)*
Gen. Colin Mackenzie

10th Royal Veteran Battn *(re-numbered as 4th, June 1815)* Gen. Lord Muncaster

11th Royal Veteran Battn *(disbanded Aug–Nov. 1814)*
Gen. Andrew J. Drummond

12th Royal Veteran Battn *(disbanded Julv 1814)*
Lt. Gen. George Benson

13th Royal Veteran Battn *(re-numbered as 7th, June 1815)*
Maj. Gen. William Raymond

Royal Newfoundland Fencibles
Maj. Gen. Sir William Henry Pringle

Nova Scotia Fencibles Lt. Gen. F.A. Wetherall

Canadian Fencibles Lt. Gen. Thomas Peter

Glengarry Light Infantry Fencibles
Maj. Gen. Edward Baynes

1st Provisional Battn of Militia *(disbanded 1814)*
Lt. Col. Commandant: Marquess of Buckingham

2nd Provisional Battn of Militia *(disbanded 1814)*
Lt. Col. Commandant: Edward Bayly

3rd Provisional Battn of Militia *(disbanded 1814)*
Lt. Col. Commandant: Sir Watkin Williams Wynn Bt.

King's German Legion
Colonel-in-Chief: Field Marshal Duke of Cambridge

KGL 1st Light Dragoons
Lt. Gen. Count Wallmoden Gimborn;
from 15 June 1815, Maj. Gen. Sir William Dörnberg

KGL 2nd Light Dragoons
Maj. Gen. John Augustus, Baron Veltheim

KGL 1st Hussars
Lt. Gen. Charles Christian, Baron Linsingen

KGL 2nd Hussars Maj. Gen. Victor, Baron Alten

KGL 3rd Hussars Col. Frederick, Baron Arentsschildt

KGL 1st Light Battn Maj. Gen. Charles, Baron Alten

KGL 2nd Light Battn Maj. Gen. Colin Halkett

KGL 1st Line Battn Field Marshal Duke of Cambridge

KGL 2nd Line Battn Maj. Gen. Adolphus, Baron Barsse

KGL 3rd Line Battn Maj. Gen. Henry de Hinuber

KGL 4th Line Battn Maj. Gen. Siegesmund, Baron Löw

KGL 5th Line Battn Col. Christian, Baron von Ompteda;
from 20 June 1815, Col. Lewis von dem Bussche

KGL 6th Line Battn Maj. Gen. Augustus von Honstedt

KGL 7th Line Battn Lt. Gen. Frederick, Baron Drechsel

KGL 8th Line Battn Maj. Gen. Peter J. Du Plat

KGL Artillery Lt. Gen. Frederick, Baron von der Decken

Brunswick Oels Corps
Colonel-in-Chief: Duke of Brunswick Oels

Brunswick Hussars Maj. Gen. Sir William Dörnberg

Roll's Regt Maj. Gen. Francis, Baron Rottenburgh

Dillon's Regt Col. Edward Dillon

Meuron's Regt Maj. Gen. George T. Walker

Watteville's Regt Maj. Gen. L. de Watteville

Chasseurs Britanniques Lt. Gen. J. Ramsay

York Light Infantry Volunteers
Lt. Gen. Sir Alexander Campbell

Royal Corsican Rangers Maj. Gen. Sir Hudson Lowe

Sicilian Regt Lt. Gen. Ronald Ferguson

1st Duke of York's Greek Light Infantry
Maj. Gen. John Oswald

2nd Greek Light Infantry Lt. Col. Richard Church

Foreign Veteran Battn
Col. Claus Benedictus, Baron von der Decken

APPENDIX 2

Militia Regiments

In 1803–33 order of precedence, with full titles

1. Berwick, Haddington, Linlithgow and Peebles
2. King's Own Staffordshire *('King's Own' from 1805)*
3. Shropshire
4. Royal Denbigh Rifle Corps *('Royal' from 1804, Light Infantry from 1809, Rifle Corps from 1813)*
5. Ross, Caithness, Sutherland and Cromarty
6. Royal Cheshire
7. Royal North Gloucestershire
   Royal South Gloucestershire

8. Wiltshire
9. 1st Somersetshire
   2nd Somersetshire
10. Inverness, Banff, Elgin and Nairn
11. Forfar and Kincardine
12. Oxfordshire
13. Bedfordshire
14. North Lincolnshire
    South Lincolnshire

15. North Hampshire
    South Hampshire (*Light Infantry from 1811*)
    Hampshire (Isle of Wight)
16. Royal Carnarvon Rifle Corps (*'Royal' from 1804, Light Infantry from 1810, Rifle Corps from 1812*)
17. Royal Westmoreland (*'Royal' from 1804, but perhaps earlier*)
18. Royal Monmouth and Brecon (*'Royal' from 1804*)
19. Royal Flint Rifle Corps (*'Royal' 1804, Fusiliers 1805, Light Infantry 1806, Rifle Corps from 1812*)
20. Royal East Middlesex
    Royal West Middlesex
    Royal Middlesex (Westminster)
21. Kirkcudbright and Wigton Light Infantry
22. Renfrew
23. Royal Radnor Light Infantry (*'Royal' from 1804, Light Infantry from 1810*)
24. Cambridge
25. Durham
26. Royal Montgomery Light Infantry (*'Royal' from 1804, Light Infantry from 1810*)
27. Royal Cardigan Rifle Corps (*'Royal' 1804, Light Infantry 1810, Rifle Corps 1812*)
28. Stirling, Dumbarton, Clackmannan and Kinross
29. Northampton
30. East Essex
    West Essex
31. Royal Cornwall Light Infantry (*Light Infantry from 1810*)
32. 1st West York
    2nd West York
    3rd West York
33. Hertfordshire
34. Fifeshire
35. Royal Cornwall and Devon Miners Light Infantry (*Light Infantry from 1813*)
36. Leicestershire
37. Royal Berkshire
38. Prince Regent's Royal Regiment of Ayr (*'Prince Regent's Royal' from 1813*)
39. Royal Carmarthen Fusiliers (*Fusiliers from 1803*)
40. Warwickshire
41. 1st Royal Surrey
    2nd Royal Surrey
42. Royal Glamorgan Light Infantry (*'Royal' from 1804, Light Infantry from 1812*)
43. Argyll and Bute
44. North York Light Infantry
45. Royal Lanarkshire
46. 1st or West Norfolk
    2nd or East Norfolk
47. Worcestershire
48. Sussex
49. King's Own Royal Buckinghamshire
50. Dorsetshire
51. Edinburgh City and County
52. lst Royal Lancashire
    2nd Royal Lancashire
    3rd or Prince Regent's Own Royal Lancashire (*'Prince Regent's Own' from 1813*)
53. Royal Cumberland (*'Royal' from 1804*)
54. Royal Pembrokeshire Rifle Corps (*'Royal' from 1804, Fusiliers from 1808, Light Infantry from 1810, Rifle Corps from 1811*)
55. Aberdeenshire
56. 1st Royal Tower Hamlets
    2nd Royal Tower Hamlets
57. East Kent
    West Kent
58. Royal East London (*'Royal' from 1804*)
    Royal West London (*'Royal' from 1804*)
59. East Suffolk
    West Suffolk
60. Northumberland Light Infantry
61. Herefordshire
62. Derbyshire
63. Rutland Light Infantry (*Light Infantry from 1810*)
64. Huntingdonshire
65. Royal Merioneth Light Infantry (*'Royal' from 1804, Light Infantry from 1810*)
66. 1st or East Devon
    2nd or North Devon
    3rd or South Devon
67. York East Riding
68. Royal Perth (*'Royal' from 1804*)
69. Royal Anglesey Light infantry (*'Royal' from 1804, Light Infantry from 1810*)
70. Dumfries, Roxburgh and Selkirk
71. Nottinghamshire

Irish Militia
In order of precedence

1. Monaghan
2. Tyrone
3. North Mayo
4. Kildare
5. Louth
6. Westmeath
7. Antrim
8. Armagh
9. Royal South Down
10. Leitrim
11. Galway
12. Royal Dublin (City)
13. Limerick City
14. Kerry
15. Longford
16. Londonderry
17. Royal Meath
18. Cavan
19. King's County
20. Kilkenny
21. Royal Limerick County
22. Sligo
23. Carlow
24. Royal North Down
25. Queen's County
26. Clare
27. Cork City
28. Tipperary (*or Duke of Clarence's Munster*)
29. Fermanagh
30. South Mayo
31. Roscommon
32. South Cork
33. Waterford Light Infantry
34. North Cork
35. Dublin County
36. Donegal
37. Wicklow
38. Wexford

Bibliography

The references listed below concentrate more upon the organisation and uniforms of the British Army than upon its campaigns. In addition to books, a number of articles are listed in cases where they have a particular bearing upon the uniforms of the army, or are of especial relevance to Charles Hamilton Smith and his work. These include the location of articles concerned with, or illustrating, individual plates from *Costume of the Army* that were reproduced in the *Journal of the Society for Army Historical Research* (abbreviated below as *JSAHR*); these details may also be found in the Army Museums Ogilby Trust's publication, *Index to British Military Costume Prints 1500-1914*, London 1972. Articles concerned especially with Charles Hamilton Smith are identified with an asterisk (*) in the following list.

Barthorp, M., *British Cavalry Uniforms since 1660*, Poole 1984

Barthorp, M., *British Infantry Uniforms since 1660*, Poole 1982

Buckley, R.M., *Slaves in Red Coats: the British West India Regiments 1795–1815*, New Haven & London 1979

Campbell, D.A., *Dress of the Royal Artillery*, London 1971

Carman, W.Y., *British Military Uniforms from Contemporary Pictures*, London 1957 (includes some examples of Hamilton Smith's watercolours)

Carman, W.Y., *Indian Army Uniforms: Cavalry*, London 1961

Carman, W.Y., *Indian Army Uniforms: Infantry*, London 1969

Carman, W.Y., 'Infantry Clothing Regulations, 1802', in *JSAHR* Vol. XIX (1940), pp. 200–35

*Carman, W.Y., 'The Cavalry Staff Corps', in *JSAHR* Vol. XLVII (1969), pp. 33–34

*Carman, W.Y., 'The Rocket Brigade in the Early 19th Century', in *JSAHR* Vol. XLI (1963), pp. 167–70

Chartrand, R., *British Forces in North America 1793–1815*, London 1998

Chartrand, R., *British Forces in the West Indies 1793–1815*, London 1996

*Chartrand, R., 'The United States Forces of 1812–1816 as drawn by Charles Hamilton Smith, Officer and Spy', in *Military Collector and Historian* (Journal of the Company of Military Historians, Washington DC), Vol. XXXV (1983), pp. 142–50

Dawnay, Maj. N.P., *The Distinction of Rank of Regimental Officers 1684 to 1855*, London 1960

Dawnay, Maj. N. P., 'The Staff Uniform of the British Army, 1767 to 1855', in *JSAHR* Vol. XXXI, pp. 64–84, 96–109

Dawnay, Maj. N.P., *The Standards, Guidons and Colours of the Household Division 1660–1973*, Tunbridge Wells 1975

Fletcher, I., *The Napoleonic Wars: Wellington's Army*, London 1996 (uniforms and equipment)

Fletcher, I., *Wellington's Foot Guards*, London 1994

Fletcher, I., *Wellington's Regiments: the Men and their Battles, from Rolica to Waterloo, 1808–1815*, Staplehurst 1994

Fortescue, Hon. Sir John, *History of the British Army*, London 1899–1920.

Fortescue, Hon. Sir John, *The County Lieutenancies and the Army, 1803–1814*, London 1909

Fosten, B., *Wellington's Heavy Cavalry*, London 1982

Fosten, B., *Wellington's Infantry, I*, London 1981

Fosten, B., *Wellington's Infantry, II*, London 1982

Fosten, B., *Wellington's Light Cavalry*, London 1982

Gates, D., *The British Light Infantry Arm, 1790–1815*, London 1987

Glover, M., *Wellington's Army in the Peninsula*, Newton Abbott 1977

Glover, R., *Peninsular Preparation: The Reform of the British Army 1795–1809*, Cambridge 1963; reprinted Trotman, Cambridge 1988

Guy, A.J., (ed)., *The Road to Waterloo: The British Army and the Struggle against Revolutionary and Napoleonic France, 1793–1815*, London 1990

Haythornthwaite, P.J., *British Cavalryman 1792–1815*, London 1994

Haythornthwaite, P.J., *British Infantry in the Napoleonic Wars*, London 1987

Haythornthwaite, P.J., *The Armies of Wellington*, London 1994

Haythornthwaite, P.J., *Wellington's Military Machine*, Tunbridge Wells 1989

Haythornthwaite, P.J. *Wellington's Specialist Troops*, London 1988

Lawson, C.C.P., *History of the Uniforms of the British Army*: Vols. IV, London 1966, and V, London 1967

McAnally, Sir Henry, *The Irish Militia 1793–1816: A Social and Military Study*, Dublin and London 1949

Mollo, B., *The Indian Army*, Poole 1981

Mollo, J., *Waterloo Uniforms: British Cavalry*, London 1973

*North, Lt. Col. R.E.F.G., 'The King's German Legion', in *JSAHR* Vol. XXXIX (1960), p. 167

Oman, Sir Charles, *History of the Peninsular War*, Oxford 1902–30; reprinted Greenhill Books, London 1995 (still a standard work on the subject)

Oman, Sir Charles, *Wellington's Army*, London 1912; reprinted Greenhill Books, London 1993

Parkyn, Maj. H.G., *Shoulder-Belt Plates and Buttons*, Aldershot 1956

Pivka, O. von, *Brunswick Troops 1809–15*, London 1985

Reid, S., *Wellington's Highlanders*, London 1992

Rogers, Col. H.C.B., *Wellington's Army*, London 1979

Strachan, H., *British Military Uniforms 1768–96: the Dress of the British Army from Official Sources*, London 1975 (includes the 1768 Clothing Warrant)

*Sumner, Revd. P., 'A Special Copy of Hamilton Smith', in *JSAHR* Vol. XXVIII (1950), p. 14

*Sumner, Revd. P., 'Drum-Major and Pioneer, 66th Foot, 1815', in *JSAHR* Vol XXII (1943), p. 131

*Sumner, Revd. P., 'Hamilton Smith's Drawings', in *JSAHR* Vol. XX (1941), pp. 85–92 (important article containing much from *An Epitome of Drawings made between the Years 1809 and 1859 by the late Lieutenant Colonel Hamilton Smith*)

Sumner, Revd. P., 'Officers' Dress Regulations 1811', in *JSAHR* Vol. XXII (1944), pp. 339–40

*Tylden, Maj. G., 'Fire Effect', in *JSAHR* XX (1941), pp. 201–04 (includes details of Hamilton Smith's experiments with coloured targets, described in more detail by Hamilton Smith himself in *The Aide-Memoire to the Military Sciences*, London 1846–52, Vol. I)

*Tylden, Maj. G., 'Sir Richard Church, KCH, and the Greek Light Infantry, 1810 to 1816', in *JSAHR* Vol. XLI (1963), pp. 159–61

*Tylden, Maj. G., 'The York Light Infantry Volunteers, 1803 to 1817', in *JSAHR* Vol. XXXIX (1960), pp. 140–43

*Tylden, Maj. G., 'The West India Regiments 1795 to 1927', in *JSAHR* Vol. XL (1962), pp. 42–9

Ward, S.G.P., *Wellington's Headquarters*, London 1957.

SATURDAY, 10TH. MARCH 2007.

SATURDAY, 10TH. MARCH 2007.